Bears &
Other Carnivores

A TIME-LIFE TELEVISION BOOK

Produced in Association with Vineyard Books, Inc.

Editor: Eleanor Graves
Series Editor: Charles Osborne
Senior Consultant: Lucille Ogle
Text Editor: Richard Oulahan
    Associate Text Editors: Bonnie Johnson, Peter Ainslie
    Author: Ogden Tanner
    Assistant Editor: Regina Grant Hersey
    Literary Research: Ellen Schachter
    Text Research: M. Caputineau-Minden, Susan R. Costello
    Copy Editors: Robert J. Myer, Greg Weed
Picture Editor: Richard O. Pollard
    Picture Research: Judith Greene
    Permissions: Cecilia Waters
Book Designer and Art Director: Jos. Trautwein
    Art Assistant: Carl Van Brunt
Production Coordinator: Jane L. Quinson

WILD, WILD WORLD OF ANIMALS
TELEVISION PROGRAM
Producers: Jonathan Donald and Lothar Wolff

This Time-Life Television Book is published by
Time-Life Films, Inc.

Bruce L. Paisner, *President*
J. Nicoll Durrie, *Business Manager*

THE AUTHOR

OGDEN TANNER, a former senior editor of TIME-LIFE Books, writes on nature and other subjects. In addition to articles on coyotes and the man-altered environment, he is the author of books in the TIME-LIFE Books American Wilderness series, *New England Wilds* and *Urban Wilds*. A native New Yorker and an architectural graduate of Princeton University, he has been a feature writer for the San Francisco *Chronicle*, associate editor of *House & Home* and assistant managing editor of *Architectural Forum*.

THE CONSULTANTS

WILLIAM G. CONWAY, General Director of the New York Zoological Society, is an internationally known zoologist with a special interest in wildlife conservation. He is on the boards of a number of scientific and conservation organizations, including the U. S. Appeal of the World Wildlife Fund and the Cornell Laboratory of Ornithology. He is a past president of the American Association of Zoological Parks and Aquariums.

DR. JAMES W. WADDICK, Curator of Education of the New York Zoological Society, is a herpetologist specializing in amphibians. He has written for many scientific journals and has participated in expeditions to Mexico, Central America and Ecuador. He is a member of the American Society of Ichthyologists and Herpetologists, a Fellow of the American Association of Zoological Parks and Aquariums and a member of its Public Education Committee.

JAMES G. DOHERTY, as Curator of Mammals for the New York Zoological Society, supervises the mammal collection of approximately 1,000 specimens at the Society's Zoological Park in the Bronx, New York. He is the author of many articles on the natural history, captive breeding and management of mammals. He is a member of the American Association of Mammalogists and a Fellow of the American Association of Zoological Parks and Aquariums.

Mark MacNamara is Assistant Curator of Mammals at the New York Zoological Society.

Wild, Wild World of Animals

Bears & Other Carnivores

Based on the television series
Wild, Wild World of Animals

Published by
TIME-LIFE FILMS

Contents

Introduction
by Ogden Tanner

A HALF-TON POLAR BEAR CRAWLS STEALTHILY across an Arctic ice floe, its small eyes fixed on a plump, unsuspecting seal. A pack of timber wolves bounds through the deep snow of a Canadian forest, nimbly avoiding the slashing hooves of an enfeebled old bull moose and closing in for the kill. A group of hyenas races after a herd of zebras on the African savanna, lunging at the legs of a laggard youngster that will soon be their victim. A tiny least weasel, weighing scarcely two ounces, searches furtively through a Midwestern meadow, its eyes and ears alert for the telltale signs of a mouse.

Each, in its own very different way, is skillfully tracking quarry that through millions of years it has come to pursue and eat. All are predators, animals that live by taking prey; all are carnivores, animals that eat other animals' flesh. In this respect they share a great many traits not only with one another but also with human beings. Men evolved as primitive—and not very skilled—hunters eons ago, and many still sit down daily to a meal of animal meat. Unlike men, however, polar bears, wolves, hyenas and weasels must take their steak any way they can find it, defend it from competing predators and sometimes risk their own lives to get it.

Bears, wolves—and other wild dogs—hyenas and weasels make up four groups of carnivores that are related in their evolutionary descent from the miacid, a creature that lived 50 million years ago.

They have certain attributes in common. All have keen senses with which to detect their prey, particularly an acute sense of smell that is most marked in wolves and is at least a hundred times more sensitive than that of man. Most are relatively intelligent, resourceful animals with large, well-developed brains. Large-eared, night-prowling animals such as foxes also have fine hearing and eyes constructed to see especially well in the dark. Most have the agility, coupled with speed or strength, to overcome their prey once they have flushed it, as well as jaws, teeth or claws capable of gripping and tearing flesh. Those that rely most heavily on meat in their diet have large daggerlike canine teeth for stabbing and holding, backed up by blade-shaped teeth that chop and shear. Since these animals do not need to chew quantities of vegetable matter for their nourishment, their rear molars are not well developed. Their simple stomachs are designed to handle the easily digested, energy-rich flesh of other animals.

Beyond these basic attributes the terrestrial carnivores have branched out widely and at times bewilderingly on the evolutionary tree, each shaped by the particular environment it lives in, the kind of food available and competition from other carnivores. As a result, each has specialized equipment, habits, camouflage and hunting skills. The weasel group, over the course of about 35 million years, has developed a broad variety of highly differentiated species. Mink and river otters, for instance, live near lakes and streams and can swim and dive expertly in pursuit of muskrats or fish; others, like martens and fishers, can climb quickly and leap from limb to limb to chase squirrels through the trees.

8

Brown bear and cub in Alaska

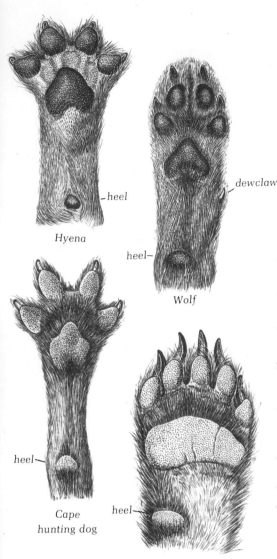

Hyena

heel

dewclaw

heel

Wolf

heel

Cape
hunting dog

heel

American black bear

A paw tells a good deal about how an animal gets its food. All the paws shown above except for those of the bear belong to hunters that rely on speed and endurance to catch their prey. Some canids, such as the wolf, race along on only four of their toes; the fifth, or "dewclaw," hangs from the side of the leg. In the Cape hunting dog, this vestigial thumb has disappeared entirely, and the paw is very much like the hyena's, whose hunting methods are somewhat similar. In both animals the heel, unnecessary for speed but useful as a brake, is placed well up the leg. The bear is a relatively slow animal that can afford to walk deliberately on all five toes, as well as its heels. It paws are strong limbs that are often used to dig up roots and tear open tree trunks in search of insects or honey.

The bears, which branched off the main trunk of the evolutionary tree at about the same time as the weasels, maintained the talents of some early miacids for tree-climbing. After a period of eating meat more or less exclusively, they became omnivorous—for reasons scientists have not yet explained. The giant pandas (pages 54–57) departed the furthest from a strictly carnivorous diet; until recently they were thought to be strict vegetarians. The polar bear, with scant choice of food in the Arctic—certainly very little vegetation—became largely carnivorous and developed into an expert swimmer and stalker in order to hunt seals, its favorite prey.

Members of the dog, or canid, family, which parted evolutionary ways with the bears about 40 million years ago, retained the same pointed nose and general arrangement of 42 teeth but evolved as far lighter and more agile animals. Wolves, coyotes and other wild hunting dogs are admirably suited to long-distance running, and they are able to chase all kinds of fast and often larger prey. A major difference between the bears and their distant, canid cousins can be seen in the way they walk: one flat-footed on the soles of its feet to support its bulk, the other on its toe pads like a sprinter.

Of all these creatures—indeed of all animals—it is the dog family with which man has had his oldest and closest associations and which has stirred his deepest affection as well as his most irrational fears. Almost certainly ancient men learned from wolves the value of hunting in groups and cooperating in order to bring down adversaries and prey larger than themselves. Most probably they also began to follow and rely on packs of wolves to point the way to quarry they themselves could not smell, hear or see. As the wild dogs satisfied their own curiosity by investigating man's ways—watching and waiting hungrily beyond the circle of his campfires and sniffing the irresistible aroma of freshly killed meat—someone must have tossed them a scrap or two. In any case, the dogs learned that men tended to leave a certain amount of flesh on the ground after a kill—meat that could be easily and profitably scavenged by staying close to groups of humans. Not only hunters but highly social animals, the wild dogs were able over a period of time to transfer their instincts and loyalties to the human societies that had adopted them. The humans' sharing of food and company and a discipline not unlike that of the dog packs may have helped these dogs make the transition.

As years passed, dogs began to develop in other ways. Genetically, dogs are extremely versatile and can interbreed freely to produce new strains. Perhaps noticing that one animal with strong bones and heavy jaws was particularly good at fighting bears, or that a leaner one had a knack for driving cattle or pointing birds, men started helping the process along by breeding different dogs for different purposes, gradually refining them into distinctive and highly specialized breeds. Over several thousand generations of dogs, the possibilities and combinations multiplied astronomically. Today, dogs come in all makes, models and sizes, from bloodhounds, sheepdogs, pointers and retrievers that work for man to novel, if not very useful, show and lap dogs such as poodles and Pekingese. Most paleontologists and animal geneticists

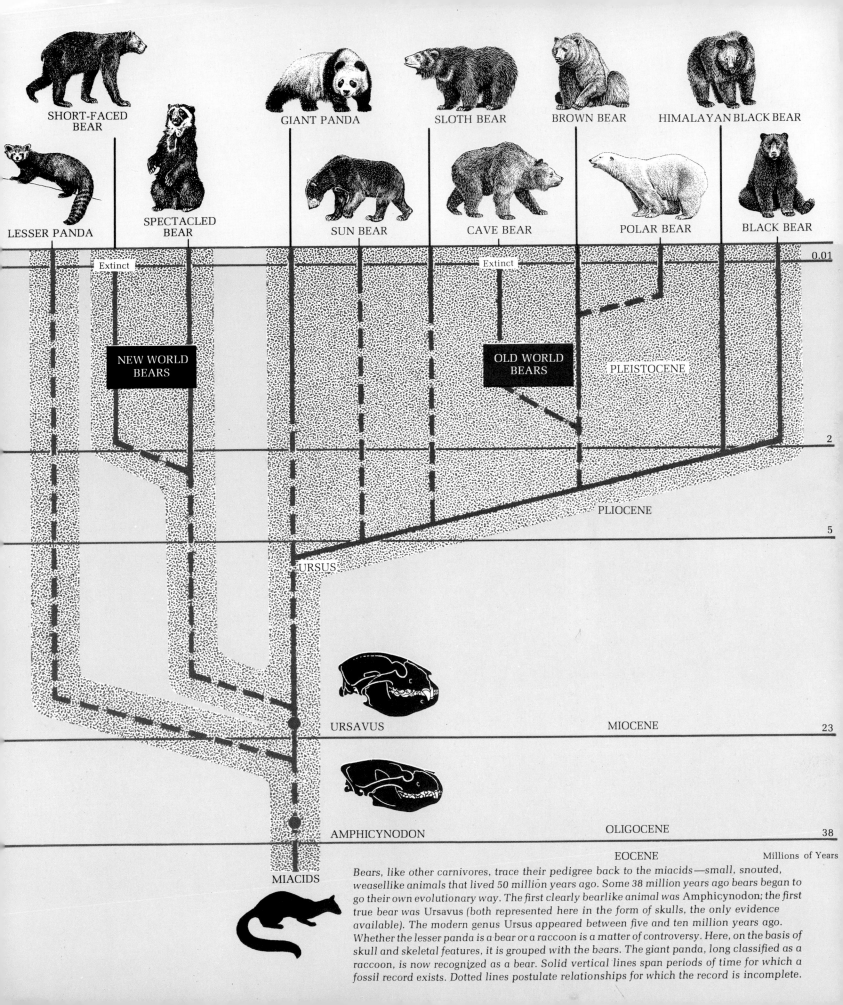

SHORT-FACED BEAR

GIANT PANDA

SLOTH BEAR

BROWN BEAR

HIMALAYAN BLACK BEAR

LESSER PANDA

SPECTACLED BEAR

SUN BEAR

CAVE BEAR

POLAR BEAR

BLACK BEAR

Extinct

Extinct

0.01

NEW WORLD BEARS

OLD WORLD BEARS

PLEISTOCENE

2

PLIOCENE

5

URSUS

URSAVUS

MIOCENE

23

AMPHICYNODON

OLIGOCENE

38

EOCENE

Millions of Years

MIACIDS

Bears, like other carnivores, trace their pedigree back to the miacids—small, snouted, weasellike animals that lived 50 million years ago. Some 38 million years ago bears began to go their own evolutionary way. The first clearly bearlike animal was Amphicynodon; the first true bear was Ursavus (both represented here in the form of skulls, the only evidence available). The modern genus Ursus appeared between five and ten million years ago. Whether the lesser panda is a bear or a raccoon is a matter of controversy. Here, on the basis of skull and skeletal features, it is grouped with the bears. The giant panda, long classified as a raccoon, is now recognized as a bear. Solid vertical lines span periods of time for which a fossil record exists. Dotted lines postulate relationships for which the record is incomplete.

These drawings show a progression in wolf posture and facial expressions from confident defiance to cringing subservience. In the top picture a dominant wolf makes an aggressive threat display, teeth bared and tail held high. The second wolf is less confident: The corners of its mouth are pulled back, its ears are flattened and its tail is lowered. The third wolf clearly shows anxiety: Its ears droop, and its mouth and tail show increasing submission. The fourth wolf shows yet a greater degree of subservience, with its tail as low and tightly tucked to its body as possible.

agree that all dog breeds now existing—from the flyweight Chihuahua to the towering Great Dane, as well as a lot of engaging mutts in between—can trace their common origins to the wolves of 20,000 years ago.

To some connoisseurs of dogs it seems ironic that the animal man regards in domestic form as his staunchest ally and companion should, in its genuine, wild form, be regarded as a vicious, slavering enemy to be shot on sight. But as humans turned from chasing prey to the less strenuous method of domesticating chickens, sheep and pigs, the dogs that remained wild, being intelligent carnivores, recognized these animals as a new food source. They sometimes failed to respect the man-made line between a scrawny, fleet-footed deer and a well-fattened, domesticated hen or calf. And so, shaken by fireside tales of wolves at the door, wolves in sheep's clothing and big bad wolves in general, settlers drove back the wilderness not only by destroying the wolves' natural habitat but also by destroying the wolves themselves.

Today there are no wolves left in large areas of their original range, and wild dogs everywhere have been relentlessly pursued. Other carnivores have been hunted and trapped too, not so much as threats to livestock but as sporting trophies or commercial pelts. The grizzly bear, once common through the American West, survives only in a few national parks, though in somewhat greater numbers in the wilderness areas of Canada and Alaska. The great white polar bear has been reduced to a population estimated at between 5,000 and 20,000 individuals. The reduction is not the fault of Eskimos, who hunt occasional bears mainly for meat, but that of visiting shooters who approach the unwary animals by snowmobile or airplane, kill them with high-powered rifles from a safe distance and, after taking skins and heads as trophies, often leave the carcasses where they fell on the ice. Only in recent years has this exceptional animal received some measure of protection through international agreements among nations bordering its Arctic habitat. Smaller predators, such as the mink, marten and fisher, though larger in numbers, have also suffered, both from commercial trapping for their valuable furs and from loss of the deep forest areas where they make their homes.

The destruction of predators, for whatever reasons, can upset the balance of nature with disastrous results. A classic example is the Kaibab plateau of northern Arizona, where earlier in this century bounties were placed on the heads of wolves and coyotes, among other predators, to protect the huge herds of newly introduced cattle and sheep. So many of these meat-eaters were shot or trapped that the deer on which they fed—generally culling out the weak, old or diseased and keeping the herds within healthy bounds—grew from 4,000 animals to more than 100,000 in the space of a few years. Their inflated numbers so overgrazed the grassland and smaller trees that in the winter of 1924–25 alone no fewer than 60,000 deer were found starved to death. Wildlife agents were faced with a continuing problem of having to shoot deer to prevent the herds from building up to another population disaster.

In many other places where attempts have been made to eliminate predators as a hazard to life and livestock, numbers of prairie dogs, rats, mice and other rodents and rabbits normally controlled by meat-eaters have soared to the point where they have begun ruining farmers' crops. To control the rampaging rodents and rabbits farmers and government agents have subjected them in turn to widespread poisoning campaigns—only to find that they were also poisoning still more coyotes, foxes, badgers and weasels that could have been keeping the pests under control. In recent years the lesson has begun to sink in that predators are not by nature "cruel, dirty killers," as some people have made them out to be, but simply creatures going about their business of hunting and eating and in the process weeding out excess animals and helping to maintain the intricate web of life. The notion also began to dawn that the predator called man, for all his shotguns, traps and chemicals, could dominate nature only at considerable long-range peril to himself.

In quite different ways, two North American animals in particular illustrate the range and intricacy of the problem: the coyote and the black-footed ferret. The coyote has so far not only managed to survive decades of all-out warfare against it but has turned into a more widespread and probably even cleverer animal than it ever was. Coyotes are not specialists but canny generalists; they have learned how to feed on almost anything, including garbage, and, most important, how to stay out of sight. In the face of repeated onslaughts by wrathful sheepherders and ranchers, they have taken up residence in the neighborhood of every major Western city. A large coyote, probably of northern origin, is showing up in Eastern woodlands where coyotes have not been recorded before (pages 96–97). Some hill-dwellers in Los Angeles, a city that may have as many as 2,000 coyotes within its limits, have given up trying to keep small dogs and cats as pets—coyotes eat them—and have learned to enjoy the nightly howling in the canyons. "The coyote is not living in our backyard," says a local conservationist who has managed to get the municipal government to build watering holes for coyotes and other wildlife around the city. "We are living in his."

Most Americans have not even heard of the black-footed ferret, a small member of the weasel family that, like the coyote, was once found throughout the Great Plains. Today, the black-footed ferret is one of the rarest animals in the world. Its principal problem was that it fed almost entirely on prairie dogs, patrolling their underground towns at night and slithering down their burrows to catch them in their dens. As farmers plowed under the burrows and poisoned their occupants because they ate up too much grass or made stumbling holes for livestock, the black-footed ferret also died—a victim of the poisoning and of starvation as its food supply shrank. Today nobody knows how many are left of these shy, appealing little animals with black feet and bold black masks around their eyes. A biologist who spends all his time looking for the animals has not recently sighted even one, and wildlife officials have sadly placed the species on the endangered list, along with other once numerous hunters such as the grizzly bear and the timber wolf.

13

Brown and Black Bears

The bears, or ursids, are the heavyweights of the land carnivores. A full-grown Alaskan Kodiak bear or an Arctic polar bear may stand over 10 feet tall on its hind legs and weigh more than 1,500 pounds.

Bears vary widely in size, color and habitat, but all are powerful, stockily built creatures with pointed, doglike muzzles, small eyes and ears, large claws and a slow, ambling gait that can quickly shift to surprising bursts of speed. Bears rely on a keen sense of smell, as well as curiosity, to locate potential sources of food. Some of their diet is carrion, but bears also hunt for mice, birds' eggs and insects. For a family classed as carnivores they also eat a substantial amount of vegetable matter that includes grasses, roots, berries and nuts. They will ignore angry bees to get at a honeycomb, one of their favorite treats.

The most widespread member of the family is the brown bear, which is found throughout Europe, Asia and North America. Despite its name, the brown bear ranges in color from black to yellow, reddish and even beige. In the northern hemisphere the brown bear was long feared, admired and even worshiped as the king of beasts, taking a special place in folk tales.

The brown bears that remain in the forests of Europe are generally small. Those living in the remote Pyrenees or Alps may weigh 200 pounds or less, though some Scandinavian and Russian bears weigh more than 750 pounds.

Still farther east, across the Pacific in the western United States, Canada and Alaska the brown bear known as the grizzly—because the white-tipped hairs of many animals give it a frosted or grizzled appearance—may reach 900 pounds or more in an adult male. It is an animal to be treated with respect. Though it will generally avoid humans, a female bear, or sow, can charge suddenly if her cubs are threatened, and the animal has even been known to outrun a horse for short distances.

Largest of all the brown bears are the Big Brown or Kodiak bears of the Alaskan coast and islands, which weigh up to 1,500 pounds. These giants fatten on everything from mountain blueberries to washed-up whale carcasses, but their particular prey is the big Pacific salmon that come up the coastal rivers each summer to spawn. Seeing a Kodiak bear rearing its monstrous bulk in the air to spot a likely fishing hole, one finds it hard to realize that it was born blind and helpless, an infant the size of a rat and weighing less than a pound.

Brown bear cubs, from one to four in number but normally two, are usually born in January or February; they are suckled by the mother in her winter den until April or May, then emerge to follow her in search of food. The cubs normally stay with her for one or more years, until the female is ready to mate again and raise another brood.

Smaller than the brown bears but more widespread in their native North America are the American black bears, which range from Mexico to Alaska and from the mountains of California to the swamps of Florida and the forests of Maine. A familiar tourist attraction in many national parks, black bears come in as many color variations as their more aggressive brown cousins. In the West they are often cinnamon-colored; an Alaskan variety called the glacier bear is silvery blue; the Kermode, living on Gribble Island off the coast of British Columbia, can be pure white.

Black bears are more agile tree climbers than the bulkier brown bears. In the Great Smoky Mountains of the Southeast, where as in so many other areas human activity has forced bears into shrinking islands of wilderness, the bears not only scurry up trees when alarmed but sometimes choose dens in tree-trunk cavities as high as 60 feet above the ground.

The bears of Asia and South America are mainly black with various markings and generally grow no larger than 300 pounds. The long-haired, large-eared Asiatic black bear, sometimes called the moon bear, is only distantly related to the North American black bear. It inhabits mountain forests from Afghanistan to the islands of Japan, spending much of its time in trees in search of acorns and other nuts. The odd-looking sloth bear of India and Sri Lanka, which has a long snout and curved claws for climbing and digging, feeds on fruits, sugarcane and honey. Its favorite food, however, is termites, which it snorts and sucks out of termite hills on the ground with a vacuum-cleaner roar that can be heard several hundred yards away. The spectacled bear, named for the yellowish rings around its eyes, survives today only in the high forests of the South American Andes, where it feeds mainly on fruits and palm buds and sleeps in nests it builds in trees out of branches and leaves. The smallest of all bears, weighing less than 150 pounds, is the comical, potbellied Malayan sun bear of Southeast Asia, a tree-climber, fruit-eater and nest-builder that is sometimes tamed by Malayans—with the help of liberal doses of honey—and kept as a pet.

Brown bear

Fishing Party

Because brown bears have no natural enemies and can easily find food on their own, they have no need for the benefits of group living. But each summer, at the beginning of the annual salmon run, the Alaskan brown bears around the McNeil River in southern Alaska abandon their characteristically solitary ways and gather at McNeil Falls, a prime fishing spot a mile above the river's mouth, to feast on the spawning salmon. The annual McNeil Falls gathering is the first social contact in 10 months for most of the bears, which compete aggressively (below) for the most advantageous places for fishing. In general, the biggest bears take over the best spots; otherwise, a specific pecking order awards the sites first to boars (male bears), followed by sows (female bears) with cubs, single sows and finally, at the bottom, the younger animals.

As the salmon flow increases, more bears appear at the falls. The 40 to 80 bears that congregate on the McNeil River make up the densest collection of bears on any of Alaska's rivers. But despite the crowding, aggressions wane as the bears concentrate on gorging themselves.

An Alaskan brown bear launches itself in a belly-flop (above), one of the more widespread fishing techniques used by bears. From a vantage point beside or in the water, the bear waits until it spots a fish struggling upstream and then dives, pinning the salmon against the rocky river bottom with its paws or mouth. One naturalist observed a bear catch two salmon in 15 minutes with only six dives.

A bear in midstream swipes at a running salmon. The bear may eat as many as eight salmon at one meal before ambling off to the woods for a nap.

After landing a fat lunch (right), the bear heads for shore, where meals are customarily taken. At the outset of the spawning season the bears eat virtually the entire fish, but as the salmon flow increases and the bears fatten, tastes become refined and only selected parts of the fish are eaten. By the end of the season some gourmands may eat only the salmon roe. But nothing is wasted: Gulls and less successful bears devour the leftovers.

No Time for Teaching

The mother bears that come to McNeil Falls to fish for salmon spend little time teaching cubs how to make their own catches; the youngsters must rely on their own powers of observation—and on trial and error—to learn the skill. While making sure the cubs get all the fish needed for growth, their mothers are also replenishing the vital layer of fat that sustains them through the winter.

Although spring is the mating season for bears, at least four species (including the browns shown here, North American blacks, polars and Himalayan black bears) pos-sess an extraordinary adaptive mechanism called delayed implantation, which prevents the fertilized eggs from developing—and thereby making additional nutritional demands on the sow—until she has fattened on salmon and vegetation. In the late fall, if the sow is fat enough, the eggs begin to grow, and two or three cubs—rarely one and very rarely four—are born by midwinter in the mother's den. A sow is a protective mother, though this attention begins to wane by the first or second summer, when she may mate again.

A young bear—no longer protected by its mother—tries to elude another bear by diving into the water to protect its catch. Weaned by the age of two and a half, cubs are then on their own, though it will be another half year before female cubs reach sexual maturity and another year and a half for males. If their mother mates again they may leave her partly out of fear of her new suitor, since cub-killing by boars is not at all uncommon.

A sow, carrying a big salmon, and four cubs (left) leave the water at McNeil Falls. The cubs may or may not be her own; familial mix-ups are common during this annual gathering, for though sows can distinguish their own cubs, cubs often seem unable to recognize their mothers. Most sows, however, will feed and even nurse an alien cub until its mother comes to claim it. Should the cub go unclaimed, it stays with its new mother and is treated as one of the family.

21

Kodiak Giants

By the time winter comes to the southern Alaskan range of the Kodiak bears they have fattened themselves sufficiently in the preceding months to be able to fast until spring in a cave or den. Kodiaks, like all other bears, do not actually hibernate but sleep most of the winter. Their body temperature does not undergo a dramatic drop, nor is their metabolism significantly reduced—changes typical in true hibernators such as ground squirrels and most North American bats. But Kodiaks and most other bears remain completely inactive until spring.

During their long sleep a remarkable adaptation called the anal plug prevents them from fouling themselves or their den. This plug is thought to be an accumulated residue of vegetable matter that blocks the intestines until it is expelled in the spring.

Mountain Monarchs

The grizzly bear, roaming the North American continent for the past million years, has managed to outlive both the saber-toothed tiger and the mastodon. As major targets of human hunters, however, the tens of thousands of grizzlies that once inhabited the Great Plains and the Rockies and Sierras of the American West—they have never lived in the forested East—have been reduced to a fraction of their former numbers. Today, most live in Alaska and Canada; probably fewer than a thousand remain in the 48 contiguous states, and those bears are found almost exclusively in some 10 million acres of Idaho, Montana and Wyoming.

Such is the fragile state of the creatures' future that the 1973 Endangered Species Act was recently amended to protect grizzlies like the cub shown below in Colorado.

A bison that died in an area of Yellowstone Park inhabited by large numbers of grizzlies brought together the bears at left. Just as other brown bears gather for fishing in Alaska, grizzlies often congregate around carrion, though not usually in the extraordinary numbers shown here.

25

In the picture sequence on these pages, a grizzly bear, which has discovered the carcass of a mule deer, defends its prize from a quartet of timber wolves. As the bear moves between the wolves and the carrion (above) the wolves backtrack quickly and then close in warily (right) as the bear retreats behind the carrion. Grizzlies are omnivorous, eating anything from ants to beached whales. They also feed on dead game and fish. On rare occasions they kill elk and dig out ground squirrels and foxes.

Persisting in their attempt to drive off the grizzly (above), the wolves circle beyond reach of the bear's lethal claws. Where their ranges overlap, grizzlies and wolves can coexist on generally peaceful terms. One naturalist observed a grizzly and a wolf feeding side by side on a caribou carcass. But a grizzly that decides to take over a wolf kill is almost always successful. In this instance the grizzly prevails, and the wolves (left) hurry off to look for an easier meal.

Our National Parks *by John Muir*

A face-to-face meeting with a bear in the wild is no everyday experience, as John Muir, a Scottish-born naturalist who was instrumental in the creation of our national parks, points out in the following passage. From his two encounters with bears in the High Sierras, Muir concludes in Our National Parks *that they are neither the shy, elusive animals that mountaineers describe, nor the aggressive, wanton killers of legend. Instead, he found, bears seem to be creatures of great dignity, not easily perturbed, with no urgent instinct to attack.*

The Sierra bear, brown or gray, the sequoia of the animals, tramps over all the park, though few travelers have the pleasure of seeing him. On he fares through the majestic forests and cañons, facing all sorts of weather, rejoicing in his strength, everywhere at home, harmonizing with the trees and rocks and shaggy chaparral. Happy

In 1879, when John Muir arrived in the Yosemite Valley, he got a job as a sawyer in a local lumber mill and built this small log cabin to be his home. It was, he said, "The handsomest house in the Valley." The sketch of the cabin and those on the following pages are Muir's own.

fellow! his lines have fallen in pleasant places—lily gardens in silver-fir forests, miles of bushes in endless variety and exuberance of bloom over hill-waves and valleys and along the banks of streams, cañons full of music and waterfalls, parks fair as Eden—places in which one might expect to meet angels rather than bears.

In this happy land no famine comes nigh him. All the year round his bread is sure, for some of the thousand kinds that he likes are always in season and accessible, ranged on the shelves of the mountains like stores in a pantry. From one to another, from climate to climate, up and down he climbs, feasting on each in turn—enjoying as great variety as if he traveled to far-off countries north and south. To him almost every thing is food except granite. Every tree helps to feed him, every bush and herb, with fruits and flowers, leaves and bark; and all the animals he can catch—badgers, gophers, ground squirrels, lizards, snakes, etc., and ants, bees, wasps, old and young, together with their eggs and larvae and nests. Craunched and hashed, down all go to his marvelous stomach, and vanish as if cast into a fire. What digestion! A sheep or a wounded deer or a pig he eats warm, about as quickly as a boy eats a buttered muffin; or should the meat be a month old, it still is welcomed with tremendous relish. After so gross a meal as this, perhaps the next will be strawberries and clover, or raspberries with mushrooms and nuts, or puckery acorns and chokecherries. And as if fearing that anything eatable in all his dominion should escape being eaten, he breaks into cabins to look after sugar, dried apples, bacon, etc. Occasionally he eats the mountaineer's bed; but when he has had a full meal of more tempting dainties he usually leaves it undisturbed, though he has been known to drag it up through a hole in the roof, carry it to the foot of a tree, and lie down on it to enjoy a siesta. Eating everything, never is he himself eaten except by man, and only man is an enemy to be feared. "B'ar meat," said a hunter from whom I was seeking information, "b'ar meat is the best meat in the mountains; their skins make the best beds, and their grease the best butter. Biscuits shortened with b'ar grease goes as far as beans; a man will walk all day on a couple of them biscuit."

In my first interview with a Sierra bear we were frightened and embarrassed, both of us, but the bear's behavior was better than mine. When I discovered him, he was standing in a narrow strip of meadow, and I was concealed behind a tree on the side of it. After studying his appearance as he stood at rest, I rushed toward him to frighten him, that I might study his gait in running. But, contrary to all I had heard about the shyness of bears, he did not run at all; and when I stopped short within a few steps from him, as he held his ground in a fighting attitude, my mistake was monstrously plain. I was then put on my good behavior, and never afterwards forgot the right manners of the wilderness.

This happened on my first Sierra excursion in the forest to the north of Yosemite Valley. I was eager to meet the animals, and many of them came to me as if willing to show themselves and make my acquaintance; but the bears kept out of my way.

An old mountaineer, in reply to my questions, told me that bears were very shy, all save grim old grizzlies, and that I might travel the mountains for years without seeing one, unless I gave my mind to them and practiced the stealthy ways of hunters. Nevertheless, it was only a few weeks after I had received this information that I met the one mentioned above, and obtained instructions at firsthand.

I was encamped in the woods about a mile back of the rim of Yosemite, beside a stream that falls into the valley by way of Indian Cañon. Nearly every day for weeks I went

The South Wall of the Yosemite Valley

to the top of the North Dome to sketch; for it commands a general view of the valley, and I was anxious to draw every tree and rock and waterfall. Carlo, a St. Bernard dog, was my companion—a fine intelligent fellow that belonged to

29

a hunter who was compelled to remain all summer on the hot plains, and who loaned him to me for the season for the sake of having him in the mountains, where he would be so much better off. Carlo knew bears through long experience, and he it was who led me to my first interview, though he seemed as much surprised as the bear at my unhunter-like behavior. One morning in June, just as the sunbeams began to stream through the trees, I set out for a day's sketching on the dome; and before we had gone half a mile from camp Carlo snuffed the air and looked cautiously ahead, lowered his bushy tail, drooped his ears, and began to step softly like a cat, turning every few yards and looking me in the face with a telling expression, saying plainly enough, "There is a bear a little way ahead." I walked carefully in the indicated direction, until I approached a small flowery meadow that I was familiar with, then crawled to the foot of a tree on its margin, bearing in mind what I had been told about the shyness of bears. Looking out cautiously over the instep of the tree, I saw a big, burly cinnamon bear[1] about thirty yards off, half erect, his paws resting on the trunk of a fir that had fallen into the meadow, his hips almost buried in grass and flowers. He was listening attentively and trying to catch the scent, showing that in some way he was aware of our approach. I watched his gestures, and tried to make the most of my opportunity to learn what I could about him, fearing he would not stay long. He made a fine picture, standing alert in the sunny garden walled in by the most beautiful firs in the world.

After examining him at leisure, noting the sharp muzzle thrust inquiringly forward, the long shaggy hair on his broad chest, the stiff ears nearly buried in the hair, and the slow, heavy way in which he moved his head, I foolishly made a rush on him, throwing up my arms and shouting to frighten him, to see him run. He did not mind the demonstration much; only pushed his head farther forward, and looked at me sharply as if asking, "What now? If you want to fight, I'm ready." Then I began to fear that on me would fall the work of running. But I was afraid to run, lest he should be encouraged to pursue me; therefore I

held my ground, staring him in the face within a dozen yards or so, putting on as bold a look as I could, and hoping the influence of the human eye would be as great as it is said to be. Under these strained relations the interview seemed to last a long time. Finally, the bear, seeing how still I was, calmly withdrew his huge paw from the log, gave me a piercing look, as if warning me not to follow him, turned, and walked slowly up the middle of the meadow into the forest; stopping every few steps and looking back to make sure that I was not trying to take him at a disadvantage in a rear attack. I was glad to part with him, and greatly enjoyed the vanishing view as he waded through the lilies and columbines.

Thenceforth I always tried to give bears respectful notice of my approach, and they usually kept well out of my way. Though they often came around my camp in the night, only once afterward, as far as I know, was I very near one of them in daylight. This time it was a grizzly I met; and as luck would have it, I was even nearer to him than I had been to the big cinnamon. Though not a large specimen, he seemed formidable enough at a distance of less than a dozen yards. His shaggy coat was well grizzled, his head almost white. When I first caught sight of him he was eating acorns under a Kellog oak, at a distance of perhaps seventy-five yards, and I tried to slip past without disturbing him. But he had either heard my steps on the gravel or caught my scent, for he came straight toward me, stopping every rod or so to look and listen: and as I was afraid to be seen running, I crawled on my hands and knees a little way to one side and hid behind a libocedrus, hoping he would pass me unnoticed. He soon came up opposite me, and stood looking ahead, while I looked at him, peering past the bulging trunk of the tree. At last, turning his head, he caught sight of mine, stared sharply a minute or two, and then, with fine dignity, disappeared in a manzanita-covered earthquake talus.

Considering how heavy and broad-footed bears are, it is wonderful how little harm they do in the wilderness. Even in the well-watered gardens of the middle region, where the flowers grow tallest, and where during warm weather

[1]*There is no separate species designated as the cinnamon bear.*

the bears wallow and roll, no evidence of destruction is visible. On the contrary, under nature's direction, the massive beasts act as gardeners. On the forest floor, carpeted with needles and brush, and on the tough sod of glacier meadows, bears make no mark; but around the sandy margin of lakes their magnificent tracks form grand lines of embroidery. Their well-worn trails extend along the main cañons on either side, and though dusty in some places make no scar on the landscape: They bite and break off the branches of some of the pines and oaks to get the nuts, but this pruning is so light that few mountaineers ever notice it; and though they interfere with the orderly lichen-veiled decay of fallen trees, tearing them to pieces to reach the colonies of ants that inhabit them, the scattered ruins are quickly pressed back into harmony by snow and rain and over-leaning vegetation.

The oddly shaped Half Dome was often used by Muir as a roost where he could sketch and contemplate the natural splendors of Yosemite, which he called "the grandest of all the special temples of nature I was ever permitted to enter." The arrows illustrate the artist-naturalist's theory that Half Dome got its peculiar shape from the pressures of glacial ice.

Black, Bold — and Sagacious

Though most people assume that the black bear, *Ursus americanus*, is found primarily in the remnant wilderness of the eastern United States, the animal is in fact one of the most widely distributed large mammals in North America. It has adapted to widely differing habitats and ranges from Alaska to Florida, though it favors forested regions where it can feed on—and take refuge in—trees (left).

Also contrary to popular belief, black bears have both a good sense of smell and good eyesight. Despite the fact that their lumbering gait—a result of having hind legs longer than forelimbs—gives them an awkward appearance, they are extremely intelligent. Black bears caught poaching outside a national wildlife refuge in Georgia, according to one refuge manager, show real sagacity. "They scuttle full tilt for the boundary line," he reports, "and let me make peace with the angry farmers while they swagger around inside the park as if they owned the place."

Tranquilized for ear tagging that will identify it in the wild, an American black bear (above) shows an impassive, expressionless face. Essentially shy and unaggressive—and despite a largely vegetarian diet—the black bear is classified as a true carnivore, fond of small game such as beaver (overleaf). At right, a black bear in western Canada stands to survey the winter landscape, looking for something it has smelled or heard.

Dangerous When Disturbed

Although many people do not regard black bears as dangerous animals, they can unquestionably kill human beings as readily as their grizzly cousins. The black bears' seeming lack of aggression, scientists have theorized, may be connected with their aboriginal, forested habitat.

Grizzlies, according to the theory, evolved on the flat, treeless reaches of the Great Plains. With little cover to retreat into they learned to stand and fight in the face of predators or danger to their cubs. Black bears, on the other hand, having adapted to trees and thick mountain foliage, learned to take advantage of vegetation as an escape. How-

ever, a wounded or cornered black bear—or one whose cubs might be endangered—can be a fearsome spectacle.

As large as many grizzlies, at a top weight of 600 pounds and with the cinnamon and dark-brown colorings that frequently occur among black bears, blacks are occasionally mistaken for grizzlies. The differences, however, are substantial. The black bear's head is smaller and narrower and is held up higher as the animal ambles along. Blacks also lack the shoulder hump of the grizzlies and have shorter, more curved claws that are razor-sharp to make tree-climbing swift and efficient.

A black bear tries to catch a beaver in a Wyoming stream. Like other bears, blacks are omnivorous, adjusting their appetite to whatever food is most readily available. But a beaver on land or in shallow water is usually easy to catch and is therefore a favorite food for bears. Black bears persistently travel an established circuit from one beaver lodge to another, often encountering the kind of determined opposition reflected in these photographs—and sometimes winding up empty-handed.

35

Exotic Quartet

The four bears shown on these pages—denizens of remote parts of the world—are unfamiliar to most Westerners, but their distinctive markings make them easily identifiable. The Asiatic black bear, for example, displays a necklace of white fur across its chest and a thick, long black ruff on its neck. Its medium-length body hair is jet black. The rings of yellowish fur around its eyes account for the spectacled bear's name. These golden markings vary greatly from one bear to another and sometimes extend from the cheeks to the chest. The Malayan sun bear has a mustard-colored crescent on its chest and close-cropped brown or black fur. The sloth bear has a coarse, shaggy ebony pelt, a white V-shaped mark on its chest and a protruding lower lip.

The spectacled bear (above) is the sole survivor of a subfamily of bears that once ranged across North and South America during the last Ice Age. Today it is found only in the Andes from Venezuela to Chile. The Asiatic black bear (left) sports a set of prominent ears, a testament to its good sense of hearing. This hardy animal's habitat is often at altitudes of more than 13,000 feet in the Himalayas.

The Malayan sun bear (right), found in Southeast Asia, Sumatra and Borneo, is the smallest bear, growing to a length of less than five feet at maturity. Its feet are tipped with long, sickle-shaped claws that are used for digging and climbing trees in search of fruits and insects.

The sloth bear (left) is an inhabitant of lowland forests of India and Sri Lanka, where it feeds primarily on termites and other insects. Using its narrow tongue and long lower lip, which it can extend far beyond its nose, the bear has no difficulty scooping up the tiny morsels.

37

The BEAR
by William Faulkner

Faulkner drew on a boyhood experience, as he often did in his writing, to recreate the clamorous, desperate action of a bear hunt in the Mississippi canebrakes, excerpted here from his novella The Bear. *The boy in the story was keenly conscious that, in participating for the first time in a bear hunt with his elders, he was being recognized as a man.*

That morning he heard the first cry. Lion had already vanished while Sam and Tennie's Jim were putting saddles on the mule and horse which had drawn the wagon and he watched the hounds as they crossed and cast, snuffing and whimpering, until they too disappeared. Then he and Major de Spain and Sam and Tennie's Jim rode after them and heard the first cry out of the wet and thawing woods not two hundred yards ahead, high, with that abject, almost human quality he had come to know, and the other hounds joining in until the gloomed woods rang and clamored. They rode then. It seemed to him that he could actually see the big blue dog boring on, silent, and the bear too: the thick, locomotive-like shape which he had seen that day four years ago crossing the blow-down, crashing on ahead of the dogs faster than he had believed it could have moved, drawing away even from the running mules. He heard a shotgun, once. The woods had opened, they were going fast, the clamor faint and fading on ahead;

they passed the man who had fired—a swamper, a pointing arm, a gaunt face, the small black orifice of his yelling studded with rotten teeth.

He heard the changed note in the hounds' uproar and two hundred yards ahead he saw them. The bear had turned. He saw Lion drive in without pausing and saw the bear strike him aside and lunge into the yelling hounds and kill one of them almost in its tracks and whirl and run again. Then they were in a streaming tide of dogs. He heard Major de Spain and Tennie's Jim shouting and the pistol sound of Tennie's Jim's leather thong as he tried to turn them. Then he and Sam Fathers were riding alone.

One of the hounds had kept on with Lion though. He recognized its voice. It was the young hound which even a year ago had had no judgment and which, by the lights of the other hounds anyway, still had none. *Maybe that's what courage is*, he thought. "Right," Sam said behind him. "Right. We got to turn him from the river if we can."

Now they were in cane: a brake. He knew the path through it as well as Sam did. They came out of the undergrowth and struck the entrance almost exactly. It would traverse the brake and come out onto a high open ridge above the river. He heard the flat clap of Walter Ewell's rifle, then two more. "No," Sam said, "I can hear the hound. Go on."

They emerged from the narrow roofless tunnel of snapping and hissing cane, still galloping, onto the open ridge below which the thick yellow river, reflectionless in the gray and streaming light, seemed not to move. Now he could hear the hound too. It was not running. The cry was a high frantic yapping and Boon was running along the edge of the bluff, his old gun leaping and jouncing against his back on its sling made of a piece of cotton plowline. He whirled and ran up to them, wild-faced, and flung himself onto the mule behind the boy. "That damn boat!" he cried. "It's on the other side! He went straight across! Lion was too close to him! That little hound too! Lion was so close I couldn't shoot! Go on!" he cried, beating his heels into the mule's flanks. "Go on!"

They plunged down the bank, slipping and sliding in the thawed earth, crashing through the willows and into the water. He felt no shock, no cold, he on one side of the swimming mule, grasping the pommel with one hand and holding his gun above the water with the other, Boon opposite him. Sam was behind them somewhere, and then the river, the water about them, was full of dogs. They swam faster than the mules; they were scrabbling up the bank before the mules touched bottom. Major de Spain was whooping from the bank they had just left and, looking back, he saw Tennie's Jim and the horse as they went into the water.

Now the woods ahead of them and the rain-heavy air were one uproar. It rang and clamored; it echoed and broke against the bank behind them and reformed and clamored

and rang until it seemed to the boy that all the hounds which had ever bayed game in this land were yelling down at him. He got his leg over the mule as it came up out of the water. Boon didn't try to mount again. He grasped one stirrup as they went up the bank and crashed through the undergrowth which fringed the bluff and saw the bear, on its hind feet, its back against a tree while the bellowing hounds swirled around it and once more Lion drove in, leaping clear of the ground.

This time the bear didn't strike him down. It caught the dog in both arms, almost loverlike, and they both went down. He was off the mule now. He drew back both hammers of the gun but he could see nothing but moiling spotted houndbodies until the bear surged up again. Boon was yelling something, he could not tell what; he could see Lion still clinging to the bear's throat and he saw the bear, half erect, strike one of the hounds with one paw and hurl it five or six feet and then, rising and rising as though it would never stop, stand erect again and begin to rake at Lion's belly with its forepaws. Then Boon was running. The boy saw the gleam of the blade in his hand and watched him leap among the hounds, hurdling them, kicking them aside as he ran, and fling himself astride the bear as he had hurled himself onto the mule, his legs locked around the bear's belly, his left arm under the bear's throat where Lion clung, and the glint of the knife as it rose and fell.

It fell just once. For an instant they almost resembled a piece of statuary: the clinging dog, the bear, the man astride its back, working and probing the buried blade. Then they went down, pulled over backward by Boon's weight, Boon underneath. It was the bear's back which reappeared first but at once Boon was astride it again. He had never released the knife and again the boy saw the almost infinitesimal movement of his arm and shoulder as he probed and sought; then the bear surged erect, raising with it the man and the dog too, and turned and still carrying the man and the dog it took two or three steps toward the woods on its hind feet as a man would have walked and crashed down. It didn't collapse, crumble. It fell all of a piece, as a tree falls, so that all three of them, man, dog and bear, seemed to bounce once.

Polar Bears

The largest meat-eating hunter walking the earth today is an animal known to zoologists as *Ursus maritimus,* to Eskimos as Nanook, meaning the great white bear of the North, and to millions of other people as the polar bear. This majestic creature is descended from brown bear ancestors that became permanently bleached and reshaped by the harsh environment north of the Arctic Circle. The polar bear is an excellent swimmer, with a long neck, powerful sloping shoulders, paddling membranes that web half the length of its forepaws and a thick, oily fur that sheds seawater and helps insulate the bear against the cold.

For an animal that may weigh more than 1,500 pounds, the polar bear is astonishingly agile. Like most other bears, it spends most of its waking hours hunting food to fuel its immense body and to build up a thick layer of protective fat—more than three inches thick on back, buttocks and thighs—to keep it warm in icy winds and water and to serve as sustenance during the long Arctic winter night.

The main source of the polar bear's high-fat diet is the blubber of Arctic seals, which it hunts in various ways. In spring an adult bear sniffs out the chambers beneath the ice where seals bear their young, carefully scrapes away the snow on top and then, rising in the air, brings its full weight down on its forepaws to shatter the thick ice over the chambers and scoop up whatever young and adult prey it finds inside. Toward the end of May, when warming temperatures start melting the ice pack enough to set large floes adrift, the bears catch the departing floes and ride them like rafts for hundreds of miles in quest of the swimming seals. Since they are not quite agile enough to catch their athletic targets in the water, they swim from floe to floe, looking for seals resting and basking in the sun. Polar bears have been known to paddle as far as 25 miles to reach a likely hunting place.

Often a bear must board a large floe to search out its quarry, standing on its hind legs to scan the ice for the dark shape of a seal. On sighting a basking seal, a polar bear quietly swims up to the floe with only its nose and eyes above water, then heaves up suddenly out of the sea to make the kill.

When it spots a seal on solid pack ice, the bear approaches from a downwind position, moving from shadow to shadow behind shielding ridges of ice. When the cover gives out the bear goes down on its belly and wriggles slowly forward, stopping immediately if the seal should raise its head to look around. A polar bear's ivory-white coat provides almost perfect camouflage, making it look like just another ridge or snowdrift against the ice.

Moreover, the bear knows that against the white background only its small black nose and eyes might be seen, so as it moves forward it often hides them with a paw or pushes a small clump of ice or snow ahead as a shield. Within range at last, it springs up and hurtles through the air to land on the quarry.

Despite the polar bear's awesome size, it does not live completely free of danger. Large seals, nimbler in the water than the bears, sometimes harry and nip at a swimming polar bear, and Arctic wolves on the mainland may try to separate a mother bear from her young. But though man is its worst enemy, the only animal a polar bear really fears is the walrus, a formidable opponent that is thoroughly at home in the ocean and is armed with tusks that may grow 30 inches long. If a bear knows that a walrus is in the water nearby, it will not go in. If by chance they do meet in the walrus's element, the bear is likely to be the loser. The 15-foot sea mammal often grapples its adversary from below, driving its ivory tusks their full length into the bear. Sometimes the bear has time to retaliate before the tusks kill; more than once the bodies of a bear and a walrus have been found locked together in death.

During the brief Arctic summer male and female bears meet, breed and part. In the waning light of October the female, prodded by the growth of the embryos in her womb, searches for a den where she will give birth and sleep out the winter storms. Returning to the mainland or a favorite island, she looks for a slope with a southern exposure, away from the north wind and toward the warming sun. In it she carves and packs an entrance passage and a rounded inner chamber resembling an igloo—a model the earliest Eskimos may have used for their own domed ice-block huts. She usually tilts the access tunnel downward so that drifting snow will insulate the entrance without trapping her inside. Through the ceiling she punches a small ventilation hole, the size of which she may change during the winter to control air and temperature inside.

By midwinter the cubs are born, usually two, and between her long, deep sleeps the huge mother clasps the tiny, blind babies to her chest for warmth and milk. In March or April the family is stirring, ready to make its first forays outside. The cubs stumble around and slide down snowbanks as their mother stretches her legs in the thawing snow. In another month or so the cubs, weighing 20 or 30 pounds, will follow her on uncertain legs as she ambles off once more toward the ice-packed ocean to teach them the art of the seal hunt and the ways of the Arctic world.

Polar bear

Den Mother

When the March sun begins to melt the Arctic snow, polar bear cubs emerge with their mothers from the snowy den that has sheltered them and her since December and get their first glimpse of the cold, white world that is their home. The cubs, like the set of triplets at left, have grown fat on their mother's nutritious milk. She, however, may have lost as much as a quarter of her normal 700-pound weight during the denning period. Once out of the den, she begins to search for food to replenish her fat supply.

Fish and ringed or bearded seals and their pups are the principal food, but grasses, lichens, berries and carrion supplement the polar bear's diet. As their mother forages in the distance, the cubs (below) huddle together insecurely, watching her every move. In a year or two they will be on their own, and the lessons of hunting and survival they have learned from her will be put to the test.

An extraordinary Arctic sight is this photograph of three polar bears joining forces to search for prey along the shores of Hudson Bay. Except for family groups of females and their cubs, polar bears usually live and hunt alone, like all other bears. Males and cubless females hunt throughout the year.

46

A Handy Survival Kit

Used as powerful paddles in the water or as efficient grasping and striking instruments in hunting on the ice, the polar bear's paws help insure its survival in its bitter Arctic range. The paws are tipped with long, curving claws (below) that enable the bear to grapple prey with one forepaw before dealing a bone-crushing blow with the other.

In swimming, the front paws, webbed half the length of the toes, can propel the bear through 100 yards of water in 33 seconds. All four paws have fur-covered soles that prevent heat loss and keep the animal from slipping on the slick ice floes. These built-in snowshoes also help muffle the sound of the bear's footsteps as it stalks its prey.

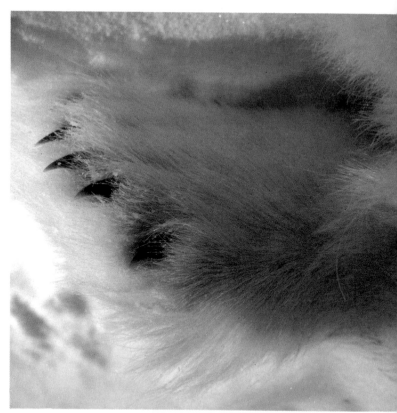

A mature 1,000-pound male polar bear has forepaws measuring about 14 inches wide. When a bear walks, the entire surface of its foot is in contact with the ground, a posture called plantigrade stance, which results in the dinner-plate-size footprints shown at left.

A polar bear paws a spray of icy water over itself. During the summer
months, when they apparently have trouble getting rid of excess body
heat, the animals depend on showers like this—and on submersion in the
water—to keep cool.

49

Rearing on its hind legs, a polar bear scans the horizon for seals. A mature polar bear consumes between 15 and 50 pounds of meat in one meal. To satisfy such a vast hunger, the polar bear may have to travel great distances, especially during the summer months when the drifting pack ice is dispersed over wide areas. One polar bear was seen swimming some 200 miles out in the open sea.

50

Pandas

Probably no animal in history has gone so far toward capturing the hearts of human beings as the chubby, clumsy-looking creature called the giant panda—darling of children, wild-animal hunters, zoo men, newspaper photographers and toy makers everywhere. Nor has any other animal quite so intrigued and baffled naturalists since its official discovery in the remote, mountainous interior of western China little more than a century ago.

The existence of this puzzling animal was first revealed in 1869 when a French missionary-naturalist, Père Jean Pierre Armand David, astonished fellow scientists by sending back to Paris a description, pelt and skeleton of a new species he named *Ursus melanoleucus* or "black and white bear." French zoologists concluded that they more closely resembled those of a much smaller animal known to occupy the same territory: the red, or lesser, panda, which looked like a cross between a raccoon and a fox but revealed its primary ancestry in a raccoonlike body and facial stripes and a long ringed tail.

For many decades after Père David's discovery the new creature—renamed the giant panda, *Ailuropoda melanoleuca*—remained among the most elusive and controversial of animals and, because of its remote habitat, a severely challenging trophy for hunters and naturalists alike. It was not until 1928 that an expedition led by Theodore Roosevelt, Jr., and his brother Kermit actually managed to find and shoot a panda, setting off a rash of expeditions backed by museums intent on getting their own stuffed specimens to display. Excitement peaked in 1936 when Ruth Harkness, a New York dress designer, carried on a search after her naturalist husband's death and arrived home with the ultimate prize—a live baby panda, which she had named Su-Lin.

As still more intrepid hunters brought back their own live specimens for major zoos, the world went on a panda craze. Welcomed in turn to Western captivity during the post-World War II years were Mei-Mei, Ming, Grumpy, Dopey, Grandma, Pan-dee, Pan-dah, Ping Ping, Chi-Chi, An'-An', Li-Li. Arrivals in 1972 at the Washington, D.C., Zoo were Ling-Ling and Hsing-Hsing, ambassadors of a historic *rapprochement* between Communist China and the United States. While people flocked to the zoos to watch each newcomer's antics, scientists were finally able to piece together a picture of the habitat and habits of this remarkable creature as it lives in the wild.

The stronghold of the giant panda is the formidable fastness of the eastern Himalayas near the Chinese-Tibetan border, a vast wilderness of jagged peaks thrusting 20,000 feet in the air above cavernous valleys and torrential mountain streams. In this land of nearly constant rain, fog and snow the panda, which the inhabitants call *bei shung*—white bear—dwells in the almost impenetrable bamboo forests that flourish on the steep slopes between 5,000 and 10,000 feet. The bamboo thickets, standing 10 to 12 feet high, provide the panda not only with cover but with an inexhaustible supply of food—succulent stems as well as stone-hard older stalks, which the animal breaks off and crunches with massive molars and immensely powerful jaws. To grasp the shoots the panda uses a unique "sixth claw," an elongated wrist bone covered with a fleshy pad that has evolved to act like an opposable thumb and that helps give the animal a comically human look as it sits back in a relaxed position, methodically bringing one shoot after another up to its mouth and getting a grip on the food with its back teeth. Because this monotonous menu is low in nourishment and hard to digest, the animals must spend most of their waking time—up to 10 or 12 hours a day—slowly munching their way through the endless thickets in order to stay alive. Although it was long thought that bamboo was the sole item in the diet of the panda, bones found in the stomachs of dead animals indicate that the species is carnivorous, occasionally eating small mammals as well as birds and carrion.

Other accumulated knowledge, including comparative blood-protein tests, has also indicated that while the giant panda branched off independently on the evolutionary tree, it is indeed closer to the bear family than to the raccoon. Like bears, giant pandas are basically heavy, ponderous land creatures, about six feet long and 300 pounds in weight, though like many bears they can climb trees to escape danger or take a nap and are especially adept at climbing when young. They live alone except when breeding, and the female generally produces one offspring in winter, sometimes two.

The panda's odd markings are still something of a mystery. According to one theory, under certain conditions of contrasting light and shadow on winter snow the black and white markings act as camouflage, though *bei shung* has few enemies to fear in its mountain retreat. Although it was once thought that the giant panda population did not exceed 40 or 50 individuals, more recent, educated guesses have put the figure at several thousand animals.

Giant panda

Bear of Mystery

The giant panda's remote and nearly inaccessible Himalayan habitat and the protection provided by the Chinese government safeguard it from hunters' guns. The inhospitable range also amounts to a frustrating bamboo curtain for curious mammalogists, who have been unable to make significant studies of pandas in the wild. Thus, most all scientific knowledge of their behavior has of necessity been based on observations of captive animals in zoos.

Since there are so few captive pandas—the Chinese government has officially banned hunting them and only rarely permits their export—the panda remains one of the world's most mysterious creatures, nearly as baffling a subject of investigation in captivity as it is when free. One highly publicized study, which involved two attempts to mate the London zoo's female, Chi-Chi (above), with the male An'-An' of the Moscow zoo, ended in failure. The Peking zoo has been more successful: At least two baby pandas have been born in captivity there.

Hsing-Hsing and Ling-Ling, the celebrated panda pair (right) that were the gift of the Chinese to the American people, indulge in a rare moment of roughhousing at Washington's National Zoo. Usually the two pay little or no attention to each other, in accordance with the asocial behavior pattern of their species.

Eating is the primary activity of pandas during their waking hours, and bamboo is their principal food—as the pair below, at the Canton zoo, greedily demonstrates. To protect them from the sharp bamboo stalks, the stomachs and esophaguses of pandas are lined with layers of tough, resilient tissues.

Wolves

"One day," wrote biologist David Mech, "I watched a long line of wolves heading along the frozen shoreline of Isle Royale, in Lake Superior. Suddenly they stopped and faced upwind toward a large moose. After a few seconds, the wolves assembled closely, wagged their tails, and touched noses. Then they started upwind single file toward the moose."

In those four sentences Mech, who has made the study of wolves his life's work, reveals more about the true nature of his subject than a hundred old trappers' stories. For wolves are not the lone, dangerous or vicious creatures of legend. They are simply the largest wild members of the dog family, and of all animals they are among the most intelligent and best adapted to living in groups. Their social organization, in fact, is remarkably close to that of man, with its reliance on individual rank and leadership, cooperation, work and play, and mutual care and training of the young. One experienced wolf watcher described a wolf's outstanding characteristic as "friendliness." Wolves form strong attachments to other members of their pack and constantly demonstrate their affection with tail-wagging, nose-licking and other gestures and sounds that serve to maintain a well-knit unit for hunting and defense.

The wolf's only major problem is man. Like other predators, it must kill animals to stay alive, hunting big game such as deer, moose, caribou, elk and mountain sheep. Because the wolf came into direct competition with human hunters for such prey—and at the same time discovered that man's well-fed cattle, sheep and pigs made good eating too—it has been systematically exterminated over great areas of its original range. In North America, where *Canis lupus* once roamed the continent from the Arctic Circle to southern Mexico, the only sizable populations left are in Canada and Alaska, with perhaps 25,000 each, plus a handful in northern Minnesota. A few hundred small red wolves, some of which have crossbred with coyotes, remain in remote pockets of Louisiana and Texas.

The wolf varies from nearly black-colored members among timber wolves in the dark Canadian forests to the almost white tundra wolves of the open, white-capped north. Adult males are about six feet long from nose to tail tip and average 95 to 100 pounds; females are about six inches shorter and 10 to 15 pounds lighter. Following the general rule that animals tend to be larger in northern habitats, Alaskan wolves have been reported to weigh as much as 175 pounds. All wolves have sensitive noses that can pick up a scent over a mile away, strong legs that can carry them at a steady trot for 40 miles a day with a top speed, in short bursts, of 35 miles an hour or more.

Wolf packs may consist of a single pair of animals or as many as 36, though the average pack is closer to six or eight. The typical pack resembles a closely knit family, which it usually is: a mated male and female, who share the leadership of the hunt and the raising of pups, joined by several of their older offspring. Discipline is maintained by a strict social hierarchy in which each member knows its place. Conflicts are settled by threatening gestures and growls as reminders of rank. If a serious fight breaks out, several wolves may gang up on one of the participants to restore order before crippling injury results.

In summer a wolf pack hunts mainly at night and rests during the heat of the day, but in winter when food is scarcer a hungry pack is likely to be hunting either by day or night. When quarry is scented, the slow, quiet stalking begins, followed at close quarters by a sudden rush. A 1,000-pound bull moose is a formidable opponent when he stands his ground and charges out with slashing hooves. The wolves know it. They wait to see if the moose will turn and flee, and then if he does, they set off to try to bring him down on the run when he is less capable of fighting back. More often the pack will single out an easier target—a gangling moose calf or a lame, sick or aged animal.

Like most other predators, wolves have to work hard for their food. In one study, of the 131 moose detected by a pack, seven were attacked and caught and only six were killed; the others were able to hold their ground or run fast and long enough so that the pack eventually gave up the chase. After a successful kill an adult wolf will eat as much as 20 or 30 pounds of meat, knowing that it may have to go without eating at all for the next several days.

After a successful chase the hunters carry back stomachfuls of meat to regurgitate for the pups and the guardians of the camp. The meat arrives warm, clean and partly digested for the younger and older animals.

Following a meal the pack usually lies around resting, but one member may decide it is time for a song and, pointing its nose skyward, break into a long, soulful howl. With much tail-wagging and excitement the others run up to join the chorus. Wolf experts are not sure exactly what makes wolves howl. It may be to round up straying members of the pack, to advertise their territory to competing packs or to communicate subtle messages of other kinds. Some suspect that wolves, like human beings, simply sing when they feel like it.

A Bleak Stretch of Lupine Turf

Driven by man into some of the most barren habitats in the northern hemisphere, wolves live out their hardscrabble lives under the grimmest conditions. Even in the Arctic spring, the treeless tundra at left is a bleak place. Arctic wolves, with their year-round white coats, are easy to spot as they leave the den area to assemble for a hunt.

The tawny timber wolf with the baleful stare (below) has a somewhat—but not much—more hospitable territory in the pine forests of Canada and Alaska. Before the white man arrived and declared war on them, wolf packs ranged over most of the continental United States, Europe and Asia, in every kind of environment except deserts and jungles. Now wolves have been virtually exterminated over most of their range, surviving only in the far north except for a few scattered enclaves in the northwestern and southeastern United States and central Europe. A notable exception is China, where wolves are still widely distributed in almost every province of that vast country.

A dominant wolf demands—and gets—submission from a lesser wolf (above), while another inferior wolf in the background shows voluntary submission. Such displays are common and serve to reinforce a pack's social structure peaceably, confirming each wolf's place in the dominance hierarchy.

Status Seekers

The wolf pack is a sophisticated and highly complex social structure. Paramount in the structure is the order of dominance among pack members, which is determined early. As soon as 30 days after birth, a new litter of wolves has established—through play and roughhousing—its dominant member. Whether that individual will achieve dominance over the entire pack in the years to come depends on such factors as the pack leader's health and on the strength of intrapack rivals ambitious youngsters must face. The leader of the pack is almost always a male, known as the "alpha male"; but a separate order of dominance exists among females, headed by an alpha female.

Lower ranks are filled by mature but subordinate animals and peripheral wolves, which operate on the outskirts of the pack. Lowest of all are juveniles, which are denied true pack membership until their second year. Adult wolves, however, are an upwardly mobile group, so that each wolf is constantly probing the reactions of its superiors, ready to take advantage of any weakness. Thus, young wolves may ascend the hierarchy as they mature, while older or debilitated wolves descend as they lose effectiveness.

An alpha male, in the picture at left, is easily distinguished from a lesser wolf, whose tail always remains lower. The only deviation from the dominance hierarchy may occur when a female has given birth. In that case, a female wolf, normally subordinate to her mate, may exhibit dominance traits, briefly reversing their roles in the pecking order.

Tail aloft, an alpha male discourages the amorous advances of a lesser male toward a female (below). The alpha male and alpha female are often the only couple that mate in the pack. This behavior is a form of birth control, in which alpha males restrain lesser males and alpha females control subordinate females.

On the hunt, a wolf pack moves single file across a snowy Alaskan meadow. An eight-year study of this pack, in Mount McKinley National Park, showed that the dominant male, or alpha wolf, did not usually lead in such processions, most often leaving that role to the second-ranking male. But in emergencies, or when the pack met with unusual lack of success on the hunt, the alpha wolf took the lead. In this photograph the alpha male is fifth from the rear, easily identified by his uplifted tail—an expression of his dominance. His mate, the alpha female, is directly in front of him.

63

Hungry as a Wolf

Wolf packs live on the edge of survival; the source of their next meal is always uncertain. And despite their unceasing search for food, they fail in the hunt much more often than they succeed. But when a feast follows several days of hunger with the killing of a caribou or moose, the wolves ravenously make the best of it. They gorge themselves, rarely leaving anything but bones and hair. Such gluttony serves a twofold purpose: in the summer to provide disgorged, semidigested food for the pups and their guards at the den and, throughout the year, to sustain strength until the next meal, which may be days in the future.

Although wolves are known to feed on any kind of animal life found within their range (including mice, rabbits, fish and birds), their primary food source, especially in winter, is larger but less abundant prey, such as the moose being pursued by the pack shown below. Even though big game is harder to bring down, it is more efficient for animals the size of wolves to hunt larger prey. Chasing a mouse-sized animal uses up a great deal of a wolf's energy and, at best, provides only a bite-sized meal.

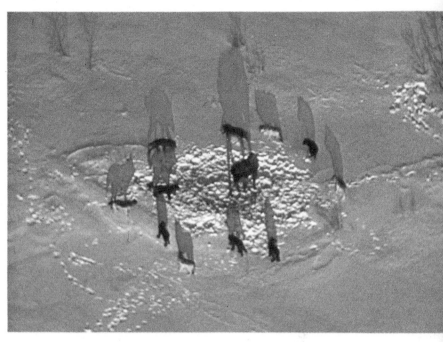

Approaching a solitary bull moose, the beginning of the abortive hunting sequence illustrated on this page, a wolf pack—one of about four in Alaska's Mount McKinley National Park—sizes up its opponent.

The pack deploys in a circle around the moose, keeping a prudent distance from the lethal front hoofs of the big moose, which discourages the wolves by standing its ground.

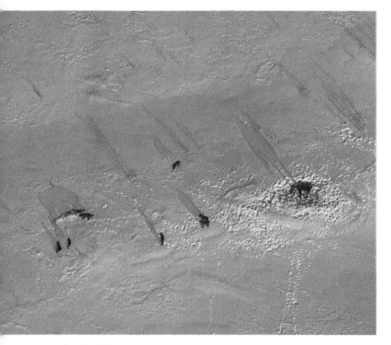

Having decided that the moose is potentially too dangerous to handle, the wolf pack abandons the hunt and, as a means of releasing frustration, begins to play.

The wolves leave the moose—though one pack member lingers for a last inspection—and take up their standard formation as they set out to seek more vulnerable prey.

A lone wolf prowls a ridge at sunset.
Such loners are outcasts—either
young animals that have been
expelled from the pack for
challenging the rigid social order, or
older wolves that have become
physically unable to take part in the
pack's teamwork. Old loners usually
live out their lives as scavengers,
following the pack at a distance and
subsisting on the meager leavings of
the pack's kills. Younger outcasts,
capable of killing deer or moose
without assistance, often seek to
change their status by mating with
other loners to form the cadres of
new wolf packs.

Never Cry Wolf

by Farley Mowat

Wolves are among the most gregarious of animals, living together in generally amiable harmony. But Farley Mowat, the Canadian ethologist, discovered a wolf family situation that went beyond the usual togetherness of the pack: a mated pair of wolves that shared their den and the chores of raising a litter of frolicsome pups with a third, adult male wolf. Mowat describes this "live-in babysitter," a patient bachelor he called Uncle Albert, in Never Cry Wolf, *a study of Arctic wolves in northern Canada that is excerpted below.*

George was a massive and eminently regal beast whose coat was silver-white. He was about a third larger than his mate, but he hardly needed this extra bulk to emphasize his air of masterful certainty. George had presence. His dignity was unassailable, yet he was by no means aloof. Conscientious to a fault, thoughtful of others, and affectionate within reasonable bounds, he was the kind of father whose idealized image appears in many wistful books of human family reminiscences, but whose real prototype has seldom paced the earth upon two legs. George was, in brief, the kind of father every son longs to acknowledge as his own.

His wife was equally memorable. A slim, almost pure-white wolf with a thick ruff around her face, and wide-spaced, slightly slanted eyes, she seemed the picture of a minx. Beautiful, ebullient, passionate to a degree, and devilish when the mood was on her, she hardly looked like the epitome of motherhood; yet there could have been no better mother anywhere. I found myself calling her Angeline, although I have never been able to trace the origin of that name in the murky depths of my own subconscious. I respected and liked George very much, but I became deeply fond of Angeline, and still live in hopes that I can somewhere find a human female who embodies all her virtues. . . .

One factor concerning the organization of the family

mystified me very much at first. During my early visit to the den I had seen *three* adult wolves; and during the first few days of observing the den I had again glimpsed the odd-wolf-out several times. He posed a major conundrum, for while I could accept the idea of a contented domestic group consisting of mated male and female and a bevy of pups, I had not yet progressed far enough into the wolf world to be able to explain, or to accept, the apparent existence of an eternal triangle.

Whoever the third wolf was, he was definitely a character. He was smaller than George, not so lithe and vigorous, and with a gray overcast to his otherwise white coat. He became "Uncle Albert" to me after the first time I saw him with the pups.

The sixth morning of my vigil had dawned bright and sunny, and Angeline and the pups took advantage of the good weather. Hardly was the sun risen (at three A.M.) when they all left the den and adjourned to a nearby sandy knoll. Here the pups worked over their mother with an enthusiasm which would certainly have driven any human female into hysterics. They were hungry; but they were also full to the ears with hellery. Two of them did their best to chew off Angeline's tail, worrying it and fighting over it until I thought I could actually see her fur flying

like spindrift; while the other two did what they could to remove her ears.

Angeline stood it with noble stoicism for about an hour and then, sadly disheveled, she attempted to protect herself by sitting on her tail and tucking her mauled head down between her legs. This was a fruitless effort. The pups went for her feet, one to each paw, and I was treated to the spectacle of the demon killer of the wilds trying desperately to cover her paws, her tail, and her head at one and the same instant.

Eventually she gave it up. Harassed beyond endurance she leaped away from her brood and raced to the top of a high sand ridge behind the den. The four pups rolled cheerfully off in pursuit, but before they could reach her she gave vent to a most peculiar cry.

The whole question of wolf communications was to intrigue me more and more as time went on, but on this occasion I was still laboring under the delusion that complex communications among animals other than man did not exist. I could make nothing definite of Angeline's high-pitched and yearning whine-cum-howl. I did, however, detect a plaintive quality in it which made my sympathies go out to her.

I was not alone. Within seconds of her *cri-de-coeur*, and

before the mob of pups could reach her, a savior appeared.

It was the third wolf. He had been sleeping in a bed hollowed in the sand at the southern end of the esker where it dipped down to disappear beneath the waters of the bay. I had not known he was there until I saw his head come up. He jumped to his feet, shook himself, and trotted straight toward the den—intercepting the pups as they prepared to scale the last slope to reach their mother.

I watched, fascinated, as he used his shoulder to bowl the leading pup over on its back and send it skidding down the lower slope toward the den. Having broken the charge, he then nipped another pup lightly on its fat behind; then he shepherded the lot of them back to what I later came to recognize as the playground area.

I hesitate to put human words into a wolf's mouth, but the effect of what followed was crystal clear. "If it's a workout you kids want," he might have said, "then I'm your wolf!"

And so he was. For the next hour he played with the pups with as much energy as if he were still one himself. The games were varied, but many of them were quite recognizable. Tag was the standby, and Albert was always "it." Leaping, rolling and weaving amongst the pups, he never left the area of the nursery knoll, while at the same time leading the youngsters such a chase that they eventually gave up.

Albert looked them over for a moment and then, after a quick glance toward the crest where Angeline was now lying in a state of peaceful relaxation, he flung himself in among the tired pups, sprawled on his back, and invited mayhem. They were game. One by one they roused and went into battle. They were really roused this time, and no holds were barred—by them, at any rate.

Some of them tried to choke the life out of Albert, although their small teeth, sharp as they were, could never have penetrated his heavy ruff. One of them, in an excess of infantile sadism, turned its back on him and pawed a shower of sand into his face. The others took to leaping as high into the air as their bowed little legs would propel

them; coming down with a satisfying thump on Albert's vulnerable belly. In between jumps they tried to chew the life out of whatever vulnerable parts came to tooth.

I began to wonder how much he could stand. Evidently he could stand a lot, for not until the pups were totally exhausted and had collapsed into complete somnolence did he get to his feet, careful not to step on the small, sprawled forms, and disengage himself. Even then he did not return to the comfort of his own bed (which he had undoubtedly earned after a night of hard hunting) but settled himself instead on the edge of the nursery knoll, where he began wolf-napping, taking a quick look at the pups every few minutes to make sure they were still safely near at hand.

His true relationship to the rest of the family was still uncertain; but as far as I was concerned he had become, and would remain, "good old Uncle Albert."

Wild Dogs

Besides the wolf, there are several other kinds of wild canids that have developed a high degree of social organization and skill at hunting in packs. One is the small, stubby-legged bush dog, which sometimes teams up in small hunting parties to pursue rodents across South American grasslands. Another is the dingo of Australia, which generally feeds on such creatures as rabbits and wallabies but is hated by herders for its raids on sheep. Still another is the fierce dhole or red dog of East Asia and India, which runs down wild pigs, goats and deer and can even force tigers to abandon their kills. Perhaps the most fascinating of the wild canids, however, is the Cape hunting dog, the "wolf" of Africa, which roams the savannas south of the Sahara in search of wildebeests, warthogs, zebras and gazelles.

To a fancier of pedigree Irish setters or collies, Africa's wild dog would undoubtedly look like a wretched mutt. Weighing about 40 pounds, the average specimen has a scruffy, short-haired coat with yellow, black and white patches, a strong body odor and a large head set off by two round, oversized ears. Unlike other canids, the Cape hunting dog has only four toes on its forefeet instead of the usual five.

But for all these shortcomings, observers who have found and followed these wild dogs in their nomadic wanderings—which cover hundreds of square miles—regard them as the most efficient predators in Africa, with some rather engaging habits that belie their looks.

Hunting dogs have a wide range of vocal effects that include a hunting call that sounds like faraway bells; a rough bark, uttered in fear or anger, often coupled with a growl; a howl, emitted with closed lips to summon the young, which peep and make mournful "mueh" sounds.

When a pack of African wild dogs starts out on a hunt, the chances are good that they will come back with bellies full. During the hot days, the animals quite sensibly stay in the shade, sleeping or socializing around their dens. In the cool of early morning or evening they set out to work. One or two leaders of the pack get up, shake off the sleepiness, then make the rounds of their fellows to roust them out. The leaders pull ears or jab with noses and paws as if to say, "Get up, let's go!" Soon all the dogs are awake and eager, wagging tails, nosing and licking, running and jumping, squeaking and yapping, with their lips pulled back in bright grins. Zoologist George Schaller, who watched this daily performance in Africa's Serengeti, described the scene as one of "chaotic, cheerful abandon, a pep rally that helped all to reach a proper pitch of excitement before they set off together on the evening hunt."

After the rally, the pack of from six to 30 dogs moves out at a trot in single file. When a herd of gazelles or wildebeests is sighted the dogs stop and bunch together and then begin a slow approach, slightly crouched, with their ears back and heads low and pointing forward. The quarry generally bolts when the dogs come into view, and the chase is on. The hunters carefully maneuver and test the herd, shortcutting or circling in an attempt to split it, watching for subtle signs that a particular animal is less fit than the others and thus more likely prey. Observers following the chase across country in a Land Rover have clocked the dogs at speeds of 30 miles an hour over distances of several miles, with spurts over 40. Inevitably a laggard gazelle or a mother and her panicky calf become separated from the herd in this race, and the dog pack closes in on them, snapping at the tender underparts and quickly disemboweling their prey.

Cape hunting dogs have been loathed for this bloody method of killing and have been shot wholesale even on some African game preserves. In reality most of their victims probably go quickly into shock and feel little pain.

The wild dog pack shares not only the rigors of the hunt but also the spoils in a generally friendly fashion, with special treatment for the young. When the younger dogs catch up with their swift-racing elders, the adults withdraw from the fresh-killed carcass and, though still hungry, form a defensive circle against hyenas, jackals and other opportunists until the pups have had their fill. Sharing continues when the pack returns to the den. The hunters are welcomed with wagging tails and happy leaps by pack members left behind—guards, cripples and mothers with small pups—and the stay-at-homes are rewarded with regurgitated chunks of meat.

Unlike lions, which seldom share their kills with their cubs, hunting dogs seem totally dedicated to their young. Male dogs spend almost as much time as females feeding, guarding or playing with the tribe's pups. In one small pack, observers noted, the lone female died when her nine offspring were five weeks old. The males pitched in and raised the youngsters until they were old enough to join actively in the wandering life of a hunter.

Cape hunting dog

High-scoring African Coursers

African wild dogs are the most skillful of the larger predators that course the plains of their continent. When a pack of wild dogs sets out on a hunt it has a 90 percent chance of success. Although wild dogs will eat almost anything, the bulk of their diet is made up of herd animals such as wildebeests, zebras, Thomson's gazelles and, at times, the larger Grant's gazelles.

The drama of a hunt by African wild dogs (in which they rely primarily on their excellent eyesight rather than their sense of smell) is usually performed twice a day—at dusk and at daybreak. Enthusiastically working together, the pack begins its search for prey. When they locate a herd the dogs rush at it and cause a stampede. Yapping as they run alongside the fleeing animals, the dogs look for likely game—an individual that is slower or weaker than the rest. If they find none and the herd has run off, as occasionally happens, they quickly call off the hunt and turn their attention to other prey. But when they do spot a vulnerable animal they attack and swiftly eviscerate their victim.

A pack of African wild dogs displays characteristic behavior in the hunting pictures on these pages. At left, the dogs nip one another excitedly until the entire pack is infused with the hunting spirit. After chasing a herd of wildebeests, some of the dogs attack a laggard (above), which kicks futilely at the biting animals as the rest of the pack approaches to join in the kill. At right, their white tails raised in triumph, the pack feasts on the freshly killed prize.

74

Puppy Love

African wild dogs are nomads that travel across vast stretches of land—sometimes more than 1,000 square miles—searching for food. Only when a female in the pack is about to give birth does the group settle down for a while. After choosing a burrow or den abandoned by another type of animal—wild dogs do not usually dig their own burrows—the entire pack awaits the arrival of the pups. There may be as many as 16 pups in a single litter. They are fed, protected and coddled by all the members of the pack, whose lives are now centered on hunting and caring for the young. When the pups are three or four months old and able to keep up with the hunt, the pack resumes its nomadic ways.

The pups at left have already developed the distinctively patterned splotchy coats of adult wild dogs. These youngsters will soon be able to join the adults in their endless search for prey. Until then, they must get their food as the pup in the top picture does, by begging and licking the face of an adult, which responds by regurgitating meat eaten on the hunt.

Jackals

Smaller than hyenas and wolves but larger than foxes, the jackals of the Old World are true members of the dog family that hunt alone, in pairs and, less often, in packs. Weighing 15 to 30 pounds full grown, they are clever, highly communicative animals equipped with excellent eyes for spotting a variety of foods. The black-backed jackal, which lives in open country from Egypt to South Africa, feeds mainly on carrion wherever larger predators such as lions leave partly eaten kills. The side-striped jackal, which generally inhabits the forested, mountainous regions of central Africa, is a timid loner that hunts for small animals at night. The most widespread is the handsome golden jackal, which gets its name from the rusty-gold shimmer of its coat. It ranges through much of Africa, southeastern Europe, Asia and northern India.

Golden jackals eat great quantities of insects, digging to find beetles and termites, pouncing on grasshoppers and leaping to snap at moths on the wing. They also hunt rats, mice, hares and ground-nesting birds, and they are not afraid to attack snakes, a regular item in their diet. Pairs sometimes team up to bring down small gazelle fawns, braving the spirited defense of a mother gazelle, which may repeatedly charge them and send them sprawling. In larger groups they also hunt adult gazelles, and they are accomplished scavengers, snatching meat right out from under the paws of feeding lions, fearlessly battling hyenas for mere tidbits in lively tugs-of-war and chasing vultures off a kill and into the air.

Jackals sometimes feast on ripe figs and mushrooms. During field studies in Africa, nature photographer Hugo van Lawick once saw a jackal pup he had named Rufus bolt down a type of mushroom that he had not seen older jackals eat. Within minutes Rufus had apparently gone on a hallucinatory "trip," rushing around in circles and charging full-grown wildebeests and gazelles, which were so surprised at the pup's wild behavior that they quickly left the scene.

Jackals, like coyotes (see page 90), are highly social animals. When members of a family are separated they communicate by howling, and when they come together after a period apart they rush up to each other, wagging their tails, nosing each other fondly and flopping on their backs to paw the air. Parents lick and groom their young often and vigorously, partly to express their affection. But grooming is an important, almost ritualistic, pattern of jackal behavior that often goes far beyond routine cleaning and currying. A jackal mother licks her pups to a degree that sometimes seems excessive. And during the annual breeding season jackal mates go into an orgy of grooming one another as an inevitable prelude to courtship.

A strange and startling quirk of jackal behavior is an acrobatic mode of combat called body-slamming or hipping—a sort of jackal karate often used to discourage competition at a kill. The animal faces its potential competitor, jumps into the air with all four feet off the ground and swings its body in a half circle to slam its hindquarters into the opponent.

The technique is especially effective in chasing off vultures or eagles. Not only does hipping serve to fluster the large birds, but by using its rear end instead of its head and teeth in the attack the jackal also protects eyes and nose from the birds' swift-striking talons and beaks. Jackal pups are quick to learn the stunt from their elders, and the more dominant members of the pack soon incorporate it into their play.

Adult jackals that are strangers to each other apparently employ body-slamming to determine which is the stronger or bolder without risk of a serious fight. Hugo van Lawick and ethologist Jane Goodall had a chance to appreciate the value of this odd performance when they watched two large male black-backed jackals approach each other one day. One was obviously more submissive than the other; he raised a paw in the air, then placed it gently on the other's shoulder as if suggesting a truce. The second animal made no response at first, but then he suddenly pivoted to smack his rear end into the other jackal. He repeated the gesture twice and finished his performance with a backward kick. Having asserted his authority, he trotted off while his opponent crouched apprehensively. The dominant animal then ran off a short distance and fetched a small piece of dried dung, which he laid on the ground in front of the other, apparently as a kind of peace offering. When the submissive jackal made no move to acknowledge the present, the donor picked it up and tossed it up in the air, then caught it before it hit the ground. As if at a signal, the cringing animal sprang up and the two began playing, chasing each other around for nearly half an hour, playing tug-of-war with a twig and ambushing each other from the cover of a fallen tree.

Black-backed jackal

A Cheeky Hunter

A brash little canid, the jackal has no hesitation about horning in, at the risk of its life, on the kills of larger animals. It is a camp-follower of man, too, trailing behind travelers or yapping on the outskirts of villages in hopes of a handout.

Jackals can also make their own kills: Working in pairs or packs, they can bring down gazelles, which they must usually defend, just as larger predators protect their kills from jackals. However, these small canids do not depend entirely on their own kills; they are not at all fussy about what they eat. As scavengers they perform useful functions in cleaning up their habitats and rank with hyenas and vultures as natural sanitation experts.

All too often jackals become the prey of larger predators; to survive, they must rely on their sharp ears to warn them of danger, their swift legs to escape at speeds of 35 miles per hour and their natural camouflage, which enables them to disappear in the sparsest brush cover.

Fending off a rival scavenger, a jackal drives an eagle (far left) away from food. As a hunter a jackal will often assail animals larger than itself (left). This Thomson's gazelle might be an easy mark for a pair or a pack of jackals but is a problem for a lone hunter. Sometimes a jackal must run for its life (below). The cheetah, shown in pursuit, is the world's fastest land animal in short spurts, but the jackal is a better long-distance runner.

Hyenas

To most people the word "hyena" conjures up an image of a cowardly, repulsive animal—a kind of misshapen, oversized dog with a shrill laugh and a revolting habit of filching leftovers from the kills of nobler animals, such as cheetahs and lions.

The only problem with this picture is that it is badly out of focus. In the first place, hyenas are not dogs at all. They are closer to cats and to such creatures as civets and mongooses but are distinctive enough to be classified as a separate family. In this family are the spotted hyena and the brown hyena of southern Africa, the striped hyena of northern Africa and southern Asia and the aardwolf, which is not a wolf but a small, shy African hyenid that eats mostly termites, usually at night. The largest and commonest species is the spotted hyena, which has a wide range south of the Sahara and is the only member of the family whose habits have been studied in any great detail.

From these recent studies, conducted in the field by the Dutch ethologist Hans Kruuk and others, a much more positive image of the hyena emerges. Kruuk and his wife suspected that hyenas in the vast Ngorongoro Crater in Tanzania in East Africa could not possibly get their entire sustenance from the leavings of the big cats, which they outnumber by almost 10 to 1, so they began following the animals on moonlit nights. They discovered that a hyena, an opportunist like most other carnivores, would eat anything from insects to water buffalo—even other hyenas. And the investigations revealed that the hyenas were actually the hunters most of the time and the lions were the scavengers, rather than the other way around. The Kruuks found that hyenas had killed at least 83 percent of the carcasses they fed on—large, healthy wildebeests, waterbucks and zebras, as well as younger and older animals. The lions simply waited until the hyenas had done their work and, attracted by the whooping, cackling calls of the triumphant hunters, moved in to chase them away and grab a free meal. Sometimes, however, a determined group of hyenas could fend the lion off.

An even more surprising discovery was that hyenas live in a female-dominated society. In tracking down its prey, a pack of hyenas was invariably led by a large female—an unusual situation among hunting carnivores, although wolf packs are occasionally led by able female hunters. A full-grown female hyena may weigh as much as 175 pounds, though the average is closer to 130; the largest males are at least 10 pounds lighter and always rank lower than the females in the pack's social scale. This extreme example of female dominance among animals was most striking around a hyena pack's cluster of tunneled dens. On the home front, as in the field, the females were in complete charge and were often openly aggressive toward the males, driving them away from the cubs with vicious snarls and bites.

The unusual social order of hyenas, Kruuk concludes, probably arises from the animals' cannibalistic inclinations. Without their larger size and aggressiveness, the mothers would not be able to protect the cubs from their own hungry fathers or uncles. During the long evolution of the hyena, female dominance almost certainly developed and persisted to insure the survival of the young. As a part of this survival pattern, one of the strangest physical phenomena in the animal world evolved. The female hyena's external genital organs became almost identical in appearance with the male's, so that it is virtually impossible for anyone but a hyena to tell the two apart. The hyena's mystifying anatomy has given rise to many myths, including the belief that the animal is a hermaphrodite or even that it can change its sex at will. Both are false. Mating and reproduction take place in the normal way.

Hyena litters are generally limited to two cubs, for unlike many other mammals the female hyena has only two teats with which to give them milk. In contrast to dog pups and bear cubs, moreover, the young hyenas are born with their eyes open and are capable of walking within a few days. To his delight, Kruuk found that young hyenas were playful, amusing and affectionate. He adopted a homeless week-old cub, which he named Solomon. Solomon loved nothing better than to accompany the Kruuks in their Land Rover to look at other animals, and he especially liked the cheese and the company to which he was introduced at the nearby Seronera Lodge, though the manager finally called a halt when Solomon started showing up in the bar. Kruuk tried to return the young hyena to his natural surroundings by locking him out of the house, only to find one day that he had broken open the front door and enthusiastically joined Mrs. Kruuk in her bath. Realizing that Solomon had become too dependent on human company to survive long in the wild, the Kruuks sadly shipped him off to a new life at the Edinburgh zoo.

Spotted hyena

Death on the Plain

Like housewives choosing the week's menus, hyenas make conscious choices of prey to be hunted on given days, varying their selection among such herd animals as zebras, wildebeests and Thomson's gazelles.

Depending on the species chosen, hyenas use different hunting techniques. In the pictures on these pages, the chosen quarry was wildebeest. When attacked, these animals scatter, unlike zebras, which tend to bunch up for mutual defense. Thus, for the most part, hyenas pursue the speedy but unpredictable wildebeests in small numbers. When hunting zebras, however—a slower but more dangerous kind of game—hyenas may band together in groups as large as 25 to make sure of the kill.

In East Africa's Serengeti Park, a lone hyena sizes up a mixed herd of zebras and wildebeests (left); the herd stops grazing to watch the predator anxiously. After a sortie or two into the midst of the herd, the hyena singles out a wildebeest that appears to be slower or weaker than the others and runs after it. As the chase continues, others of the hyena clan join in (left, below), while the herd resumes its grazing. Coursing along at top speed, the leading hyena overtakes the hapless wildebeest (below) and slows it with savage bites at its loins and rump.

As the doomed wildebeest sinks to the ground, the rest of the pursuers arrive at the scene (far left) and join in the kill (left). Hyenas usually eviscerate their victims as they catch them and literally eat them alive. A pack of hyenas will devour a wildebeest in a matter of seven or eight minutes.

A large pack of spotted hyenas hastily feeds on a zebra while jackals attempt to squirm in under their bodies to snatch a morsel, and vultures watch. After a successful kill, a pack of cackling hyenas almost always attracts swarms of uninvited guests to the feast. If the scavengers are large and dangerous, like lions, the hyenas may have to yield their prey altogether, but they can fend off smaller interlopers, sometimes killing the bolder ones.

86

Innocent Killers by Hugo and Jane van Lawick-Goodall

Spotted hyenas are tribal animals with a ferocious sense of territoriality. Whenever a strange pack of hyenas intrudes on the territory of another pack, a shrieking, bloody battle inevitably follows, often ending in death for some animals. Such a clash, led by two formidable female hyenas, is described in the passage below from Innocent Killers *by Jane Goodall, the British ethologist, and her former husband, Hugo van Lawick, the Dutch naturalist and photographer.*

Bloody Mary and Lady Astor, leading matriarchs of the Scratching Rocks Clan, began to run fast over the moonlit plain, their tails aggressively curled over their broad rumps. Behind them ran some eighteen other members of the clan. About sixty yards ahead two hyenas of the neighbouring Lakeside Clan were resting close to the boundary of their territory. It seems that they were fast asleep, for when they got up Bloody Mary and Lady Astor were only a few yards from them. One of the pair was lucky and escaped, running for its life, but the other was not quick enough. Bloody Mary and Lady Astor seized hold of it and a few moments later it was practically hidden from sight as more and more of its enemies rushed in to bite and rend at its body. The night was filled with the fearsome roars and low whooping calls and growls of the triumphant Scratching Rocks Clan and the horrible screams of their victim.

Suddenly, however, a group of ten hyenas of the Lakeside Clan materialised out of the night and came racing in tight formation towards the battle ground. This group was small, but it was within its territory and the hyenas, as they ran to defend their 'rights', were confident and aggressive. The unruly mob of Scratching Rocksters retreated hastily, leaving behind their badly wounded victim. For a short distance the Lakeside Clan pursued them, but once they had crossed the boundary into Scratching Rocks territory they stopped, uneasy on foreign soil.

Meanwhile the Scratching Rocksters, once they were well within their own territory, also stopped, and the two rival clans faced each other, both sides keeping tight formation. Each individual held its tail curled stiffly over its rump, and the low growling whooping calls sounded louder and louder in the night air. And all the time both clans were swelling in numbers as more and more members, attracted by the calls of battle, hurried to the scene.

Suddenly I saw the shadowy forms of Bloody Mary and Lady Astor rush forward, side by side, and a moment later

the rest of the clan was behind its leaders. For a short while the Lakesiders held their ground, and there were loud roars and shrill giggling, chuckling sounds as hyenas briefly attacked and chased each other in the skirmish. And then the Lakeside Clan retreated, running back into its own territory. After chasing for a short distance the Scratching Rocksters, who had once more crossed their boundary, began to feel uneasy and they stopped. Again the two clans faced each other, the whooping calls filling the air until the Lakesiders, reaching a peak of frenzy, rushed forward to renew hostilities. Another brief skirmish and then the Scratching Rocks Clan once more retreated into its own territory.

And so it went on, each clan surging forward in turn behind its leaders and then suddenly breaking and rushing back from the aggressive charge of the other. Eventually there were between thirty and forty hyenas on each side, and the cacophony of their weird calls, the rustling and pounding of their heavy feet, the menace of their dark shapes were everywhere around us in the moonlight.

Twenty minutes from the start of the affair the skirmishing suddenly ended and members of both clans moved farther and farther into their own territories, some

Eight hyena "clans" have subdivided Ngorongoro Crater into well-marked territories, each one off limits to neighboring clans, and one neutral zone (9) unclaimed by any clan.

occasionally glancing back over their shoulders as though to make certain there were no further infringements of the boundary. Hugo and I had seen a number of territorial disputes before, between the different hyena clans of the Ngorongoro Crater, but never one to equal that which we had just watched for sheer, seemingly unprovoked hostility. For, whilst the two resting Lakesiders who had started the incident may have been guilty of trespass, at the very most they were only a few yards on the wrong side of their clan boundary. What a price one of them had paid for its indiscretion, for almost certainly it would die of its wounds!

Coyotes

The coyote, America's equivalent of the Old World jackal in the dog family, has perhaps the keenest instinct for survival of all the hunters. Unlike many predators, it has adapted to the incursions of civilization, even surviving a deliberate, brutal campaign of extermination waged by man. And while the coyote population has declined drastically in some areas, the animal has extended its range. Coyotes, originally animals of the western plains and uplands, have moved into widely varying habitats all the way from Costa Rica in Central America to Point Barrow in Alaska more than 7,000 miles away. Their nightly howling can be heard by movie stars on their terraces in Hollywood Hills and by backpackers camping in the White Mountains of New Hampshire, where no coyotes existed 30 years ago. Their total population in the United States today may be about a million; their future is by no means secure.

Just what is this extraordinary animal, and what enables it to hold out against man at all? The coyote is basically a smaller version of the wolf, weighing 20 to 40 pounds, about a third the size of its larger cousin. It has thinner legs than the wolf, daintier feet and a narrower pointed nose, with bright yellow eyes and a long bushy tail. It is as intelligent as the wolf, less discriminating in its diet and more resourceful in adapting to—and avoiding—man.

Yet the coyote has an attribute that tempts people to compare it to man: an appearance of genuine family solidarity. Like wolves—and unlike domestic dogs—mated coyotes may stay together for life. And though a male dog generally ignores the pups he has sired, a male coyote dutifully helps to raise his progeny (usually five or six to a litter), guarding and playing with the pups, grooming them with licks of his tongue and bringing them back morsels from the hunt.

Hunting and feeding habits are a major factor in the survival of any species—not least in the case of the coyote. Being a relatively small animal, it does not require great quantities of meat and therefore does not need to kill the large animals that are also valued by humans. It can subsist on rabbits, mice, prairie dogs, lizards, birds' eggs and leftovers from garbage pails—sources of food that are both widely available and generally left alone by people.

Though some coyotes have an annoying habit of helping themselves to tomatoes, melons and chickens when the opportunity presents itself, the good that coyotes do far outweighs their sins. Over the years the coyote has been more friend than foe to many farmers and cattle ranchers, acting as a control over rodents and other pests which, if allowed to proliferate, would ruin grassland and crops.

The coyote's greatest enemy has been the professional sheep raiser, who for years has reacted angrily to losses of lambs and ewes, promoting full-scale war on the little wolf—despite studies that show only a small proportion of coyotes actually kill sheep.

The casualties of this war have been heavy. During a single year in the 1960s, government predator-control agents claimed an official body count of no fewer than 89,653 coyotes. Yet the carnage failed in the long run to accomplish its objective of coyote control. In a finely tuned response to the altered situation, female coyotes have produced larger litters to replace their reduced numbers.

Despite the persecution, coyotes have gone about their business, displaying an almost uncanny ability to coexist with human beings while remaining largely out of sight. Near human settlements they have learned to confine their major activities to nighttime; where people are scarcer they travel by day as well. Sometimes they hunt alone, but when it is to their advantage they team up in pairs or in small family packs of five or six. Several coyotes were once seen advancing across a field like a line of infantrymen; when one flushed a rabbit the rest immediately surrounded it to cut off all escape.

The teamwork of a pair of coyotes hunting together is an intriguing display of planning and practice. One coyote may conceal itself behind a bush while another chases a rabbit toward the hiding place and then leap out to intercept the fugitive as it runs by. One observer actually watched a coyote jumping stiff-legged in the air and cavorting before an astonished rabbit, which was so transfixed by the strange performance that it never noticed another coyote creeping up to seize it from behind.

Coyotes are clever enough to work in partnership with—or exploit—other animals. Working a highly successful version of the badger game, a coyote may combine forces with a badger hunting in the same area. The coyote uses its keen senses and agility to scare up ground squirrels or prairie dogs and profits from the badger's ability to follow the prey into their holes and drive them out—where the coyote eats them.

North American coyote

Master of Making Do

Once inhabiting a limited range in the American Southwest, the coyote has, of necessity, become a nomad. As an all-out extermination campaign in the West was threatening it with extinction, the resourceful coyote was extending its range across North America, roaming as far north as Alaska, south to Central America and eastward to New York and Maine (see pages 96–97). Perhaps the most adaptable of the wild canids, the coyote has learned to survive in the widely diversified habitats shown on these pages.

A coyote usually hunts alone, which has led to the impression that it is a solitary creature. Actually, it is an animal that forms loose bonds with other coyotes in its vicinity and a strong, often lifelong, relationship with a mate. Despite its lonely sound, the coyote's howl may be a form of communication—the animal's way of keeping in touch with neighbors, telling them of food supplies or warning of danger. The coyote also utters a sharp yip, the source of its Latin name, *Canis latrans*, or barking dog.

Extremes of weather seem to pose few obstacles for coyotes, which manage to adapt as easily to the broiling heat of Arizona's Grand Canyon (right) as to the biting cold of winter in Jackson Hole, Wyoming (opposite).

A coyote pauses in a prairie dog town on the plains of the western United States in hopes of catching one of its inhabitants. Some of the prairie dogs watch the coyote from a safe distance in the background, ready to duck into the mounds they build as refuges and denning sites.

A Matter of Taste

When it comes to their diet, coyotes are among the least finicky of the carnivores. They feed primarily on rabbits and rodents but have also developed a taste for fish, frogs and leftover TV dinners. Mice in particular make up a substantial part of a coyote's intake. In winter the coyote's keen sense of hearing helps it detect the sounds of small rodents as they scurry in and out of air pockets beneath the snow. Pouncing through the thin crust of ice (above), a coyote unearths a mouse, which, after a futile attempt at escape (left), is quickly devoured.

Coyotes live singly, in pairs and in clans, usually made up of parents and their young, although other adults may also be included. Members of the clan hunt within tribal territories that range in size from 10 to 25 square miles, depending on the abundance of food. Because their prey is usually small, coyotes are lone hunters, although on rare occasions a group will work together to stalk bigger game.

A coyote licks up a snack of insects that are swarming over the trunk of a tree (above). But an encounter with a beaver (above, right) provides a much better opportunity for a hungry coyote to make a full meal.

Two coyotes go through the ritual of establishing dominance before they get down to the business of eating the carcass of a fallen mule deer (right). After much growling and baring of teeth one animal capitulates and steps aside; the victor feeds first.

A New Habitat Back East

The largest population of eastern coyotes lives in habitats ranging from Maine to New York (light shading), with a few individuals to be found as far south as Virginia. They are most numerous in farm and woodland areas (dark shading). Their ancestors came from the Great Plains across southern Canada (inset, heavy arrow), although some may have taken a route (light arrow) south of the Great Lakes.

In New England in the 1950s a persistent rumor was confirmed: A new kind of canid had appeared in the region where nothing like it had been recorded before. It appeared to be larger than a coyote and smaller than a wolf, and it had characteristics of both animals. It looked like an overgrown coyote, with the coloration of a dark wolf. It had all the intelligence and instinct for survival of a western coyote, yet it traveled in packs like the wolf.

Some observers speculated that it was a breed of domestic dog turned feral. Others believed that it was a coydog—the result of a coyote's mating with a domestic dog. The likeliest conclusion was that the newcomer was a distinct subspecies, the eastern coyote.

Scientists agree that the newcomer probably came east to escape western-based programs of systematic coyote extirpation and that it filled an ecological niche left vacant in the east by the extermination of wolves and other large predators over the past century and a half.

As adaptable as the western coyote, the eastern coyote is at home in the deep snows of the Adirondack or Green mountains (right) and in the back alleys of New England towns, where it regularly scavenges local garbage cans.

ROUGHING IT
by Mark Twain

In 1861, when he was 26, Mark Twain journeyed to Carson City, Nevada, with his brother, the newly appointed territorial governor. His impressions of life on the western frontier, including this description of his first confrontation with the notorious coyote, were recorded in Roughing It. *Twain's distaste for the coyote was a reflection of prevailing opinion, but his accurate description of the animal's behavior revealed a true respect for the coyote's cunning. It would be a hundred years before public opinion changed, and the much maligned coyote was reevaluated as a useful and even admirable creature.*

Along about an hour after breakfast we saw the first prairie-dog villages, the first antelope, and the first wolf. If I remember rightly, this latter was the regular *coyote* (pronounced ky-*o*-te) of the farther deserts. And if it *was*, he was not a pretty creature, or respectable either, for I got well acquainted with his race afterward, and can speak with confidence. The coyote is a long, slim, sick and sorry-looking skeleton, with a gray wolf-skin stretched over it, a tolerably bushy tail that forever sags down with a

despairing expression of forsakenness and misery, a furtive and evil eye, and a long, sharp face, with slightly lifted lip and exposed teeth. He has a general slinking expression all over. The coyote is a living, breathing allegory of Want. He is *always* hungry. He is always poor, out of luck and friendless. The meanest creatures despise him, and even the fleas would desert him for a velocipede. He is so spiritless and cowardly that even while his exposed teeth are pretending a threat, the rest of his face is apologizing for it. And he is *so* homely!—so scrawny, and ribby, and coarse-haired, and pitiful. When he sees you he lifts his lip and lets a flash of his teeth out, and then turns a little out of the course he was pursuing, depresses his head a bit, and strikes a long, soft-footed trot through the sage-brush, glancing over his shoulder at you, from time to time, till he is about out of easy pistol range, and then he stops and takes a deliberate survey of you; he will trot fifty yards and stop again—another fifty and stop again; and finally the gray of his gliding body blends with the gray of the sage-brush, and he disappears. All this is when you make no demonstration against him; but if you do, he develops a livelier interest in his journey, and instantly electrifies his heels and puts such a deal of real estate between himself and your weapon, that by the time you have raised the hammer you see that you need a minie rifle, and by the

time you have got him in line you need a rifled cannon, and by the time you have "drawn a bead" on him you see well enough that nothing but an unusually long-winded streak of lightning could reach him where he is now. But if you start a swift-footed dog after him, you will enjoy it ever so much—especially if it is a dog that has a good opinion of himself, and has been brought up to think he knows something about speed. The coyote will go swinging gently off on that deceitful trot of his, and every little while he will smile a fraudful smile over his shoulder that will fill that dog entirely full of encouragement and worldly ambition, and make him lay his head still lower to the ground, and stretch his neck further to the front, and pant more fiercely, and stick his tail out straighter behind, and move his furious legs with a yet wilder frenzy, and leave a broader and broader, and higher and denser cloud of desert sand smoking behind, and marking his long wake across the level plain! And all this time the dog is only a short twenty feet behind the coyote, and to save the soul of him he cannot understand why it is that he cannot get perceptibly closer; and he begins to get aggravated, and it makes him madder and madder to see how gently the coyote glides along and never pants or sweats or ceases to smile; and he grows still more and more incensed to see how shamefully he has been taken in by an entire stranger,

and what an ignoble swindle that long, calm, soft-footed trot is; and next he notices that he is getting fagged, and that the coyote actually has to slacken speed a little to keep from running away from him—and *then* that towndog is mad in earnest, and he begins to strain and weep and swear, and paw the sand higher than ever, and reach for the coyote with concentrated and desperate energy. This "spurt" finds him six feet behind the gliding enemy, and two miles from his friends. And then, in the instant that a wild new hope is lighting up his face, the coyote turns and smiles blandly upon him once more, and with a something about it which seems to say: "Well, I shall have to tear myself away from you, bub—business is business, and it will not do for me to be fooling along this way all day"— and forthwith there is a rushing sound, and the sudden splitting of a long crack through the atmosphere, and

behold that dog is solitary and alone in the midst of a vast solitude!

It makes his head swim. He stops, and looks all around; climbs the nearest sand-mound, and gazes into the distance; shakes his head reflectively, and then, without a word, he turns and jogs along back to his train, and takes up a humble position under the hindmost wagon, and feels unspeakably mean, and looks ashamed, and hangs his tail at half-mast for a week. And for as much as a year after that, whenever there is a great hue and cry after a coyote, that dog will merely glance in that direction without emotion, and apparently observe to himself, "I believe I do not wish any of the pie."

The coyote lives chiefly in the most desolate and forbidding deserts, along with the lizard, the jackass-rabbit and the raven, and gets an uncertain and precarious living, and earns it. He seems to subsist almost wholly on the carcasses of oxen, mules, and horses that have dropped out of emigrant trains and died, and upon windfalls of carrion, and occasional legacies of offal bequeathed to him by white men who have been opulent enough to have something better to butcher than condemned army bacon. He will eat anything in the world that his first cousins, the desert-frequenting tribes of Indians, will, and they will eat anything they can bite. It is a curious fact that these latter are the only creatures known to history who will eat nitroglycerin and ask for more if they survive.

The coyote of the deserts beyond the Rocky Mountains has a peculiarly hard time of it, owing to the fact that his relations, the Indians, are just as apt to be the first to detect a seductive scent on the desert breeze, and follow the fragrance to the late ox it emanated from, as he is himself; and when this occurs he has to content himself with sitting off at a little distance watching those people strip off and dig out everything edible, and walk off with it. Then he and the waiting ravens explore the skeleton and polish the bones. It is considered that the coyote, and the obscene bird, and the Indian of the desert, testify their blood-kinship with each other in that they live together in the waste places of the earth on terms of perfect confidence and friendship, while hating all other creatures and yearning to assist at their funerals. He does not mind going a hundred miles to breakfast, and a hundred and fifty to dinner, because he is sure to have three or four days between meals, and he can just as well be traveling and looking at the scenery as lying around doing nothing and adding to the burdens of his parents.

We soon learned to recognize the sharp, vicious bark of the coyote as it came across the murky plain at night to disturb our dreams among the mail-sacks; and remembering his forlorn aspect and his hard fortune, made shift to wish him the blessed novelty of a long day's good luck and a limitless larder the morrow.

Foxes

The smallest members of the dog family are the foxes, which are found in most parts of the world. Like their larger coyote and jackal cousins, most have managed to survive, despite the encroachments of man, by adjusting their ways to a human-dominated world.

Of all the foxes, the most widespread today is the red fox, common through North America, Europe and Asia. The crafty Reynard of countless fables, it is a handsome, alert-looking animal whose long, silky fur—often reddish and set off by a white chest, black "boots" and a bushy tail—sometimes makes it appear larger than its eight to 11 pounds. Part of the red fox's appeal is its alert expression, with elliptical, catlike eyes that are unique to foxes among canids and are able to detect the slightest movement.

It can live almost anywhere—families were found in the ruins of Berlin after World War II, feeding on refuse, rats and mice—but it generally prefers open meadowland where field mice, voles and cottontail rabbits abound. A red fox's diet also includes grasshoppers, an occasional quail or henhouse chicken and, in season, wild strawberries, blueberries, cherries, apples and grapes.

Red foxes usually take over abandoned dens from accomplished diggers such as woodchucks or badgers, then enlarge them into long underground tunnels with a maternity chamber and several escape entrances and exits. (One den in New York State, occupied by two red fox families, had no fewer than 27 ways to get in and out.) The mother fox, or vixen, bears four to eight kits in early spring. Fox kits emerge from their den on wobbly feet after a few weeks. At that time, both parents must maintain a constant watch for larger predators, including hawks, cats, dogs and man. Should an intruder come too close, the anxious parents will often move the pups to another, safer den. Both adults bring food to their young and frequently bury surplus items for future use.

When the red fox cannot outwit its enemies, it can usually outrun them. Perhaps the ultimate sporting compliment to Reynard's abilities is paid by ladies and gentlemen who ride to hounds in his pursuit. As often as not the fox gives its pursuers the slip, bounding along stone walls, doubling back on its tracks, throwing the hounds off the scent and confusing the hunters.

Other foxes rely on somewhat different means of self-defense. The gray fox, which ranges throughout the United States and as far south as Colombia and Venezuela, is, along with the corsac fox of northern Asia, the only canid that is an accomplished climber; it can easily escape most followers by shinnying up the nearest tree. The small swift and kit foxes of the North American plains and deserts rely on their exceptionally large ears to help warn them of danger. When they feel imperiled they flee in dazzling zigzag dashes that few other animals can follow with their eyes, much less their legs. The graceful kit foxes in particular are great controllers of rodents. Unhappily, due to growing desert settlement and poisoned bait set out for coyotes and prairie dogs, kit foxes have dwindled in number, and they are now on the endangered species list.

Similar to the swift and kit foxes are several species of big-eared foxes, which live in a variety of African habitats. Smallest of all is the fennec. Weighing three pounds or less, with soft, creamy white fur, large, dark eyes, pointed noses and enormous ears that stick six inches in the air, fennecs are shy hunters that forage at night for insects, lizards and small rodents, as well as berries and fruits.

In colder, northern areas, foxes have evolved still other means of survival, including camouflage. The so-called silver fox, highly valued commercially for its beautiful fur, is actually a variety of red fox, with blackish, silver-tipped hairs that conceal it in the dark evergreen woods. The Arctic fox, another favorite of trappers and furriers, varies from nearly black to steely blue, light gray and chestnut brown. Where snow and ice last for many months, its winter coat turns completely white, with a few black hairs at the tip of the tail. Arctic foxes have adapted to the rigors of northern living, feeding on nesting birds, lemmings and other small rodents in summer and often following polar bears in winter to scavenge seal carcasses.

Despite the bitter polar winter, Arctic foxes are not hibernators. The only canid that sleeps through most of the winter is the odd-looking raccoon dog of Japan, Asia and eastern Europe, a foxlike creature that, as its name implies, sprouted on the evolutionary tree of carnivores looking like a raccoon.

Among other foxlike curiosities are the South American canids, a collection that includes the crab-eating fox and the pampas fox. Probably the strangest of the lot is an animal called the maned wolf, named for a dark scruff of fur along its back. Ranging the grassy uplands of Brazil and Argentina, it is a rare and solitary creature that hunts mainly at night for wild guinea pigs, other small mammals and birds. Its extraordinarily long legs give it an awkward, swaying lope. But they come in handy in the tall grass of the savanna, over which the maned wolf can easily peer to spot its only enemies, fire and man, as well as prey.

Patagonian gray fox

The Adaptable Reynard

Sighted only rarely by human observers, the red fox is nevertheless one of the most abundant and wide-ranging of the world's smaller hunters. Much of its success comes from the fact that it has adapted to a wide variety of habitats, from the tangled undergrowth of the forests (below) to the swaying grasses of cleared farmlands (opposite), from the stark expanses of the Alaskan tundra to the bustle of well-populated suburban areas. The red fox feeds on almost anything—primarily rodents but also insects, fish, carrion, grass, berries and birds and their eggs. Foxes sometimes collect birds' eggs during the spring when they are plentiful and bury them, to be retrieved months later when other food is scarce.

Red foxes are year-round hunters. They do not hibernate, although they may seek shelter for a day or two during severe winter weather. In spring and summer when food is abundant, a male fox and his family can survive within a one-mile range. But as winter sets in and food becomes harder to find, a male fox may have to cover a range of 20 square miles just to feed himself.

The Little Foxes

When they are about a year old, foxes become sexually mature. In January or February the males, which have been solitary for most of the winter, seek out a mate. Males often squabble over a female, since her period of receptivity lasts only a few days. Gestation lasts from 50 to 53 days, a period when the female readies her den (vixens often use the same den year after year) by lining it with leaves and hair. The helpless kits weigh about two to four ounces at birth. They are blind for the first 10 days and are dependent on their mother's milk for food.

As the youngsters grow, regurgitated meat is added to their diet. By the tenth week the kits are completely weaned and are taken on their first hunt. They must learn quickly to detect and elude pursuers, for at the end of the fall season the family disbands and each member goes its separate way.

The red fox kit above seems overwhelmed by the world outside its den. Kits are extremely vulnerable to predators and are usually kept in the den until they are older and stronger than this one. While the vixen is occupied nursing the kits, the male, like the one at right bringing home a bird for dinner, assumes all the hunting responsibilities for himself and his mate.

About five weeks old, kits emerge from their
burrow to begin learning how to be foxes.
Although the group above doesn't seem eager
to wander far from home, they will eventually
become more venturesome and
frisky—running, wrestling with playmates
and growing stronger under the watchful eyes
of their parents.

A vixen (right) suckles two of her young in a
characteristic nursing position of wild
canids—standing up. The kits grow quickly.
By the time they are a year old they will be
full-grown, measuring between 36 and 48
inches, including 12 to 16 inches of fluffy,
flowing, white-tipped tail.

Vulpine Variations

Although foxes share an unmistakable clan resemblance, the group can also boast an astonishing diversity of form and color. Each of the approximately 16 fox varieties—notably the six on these pages—has a look of its own.

In the top row of small photographs (left to right) the African fennec, the smallest of the foxes, measuring 16 inches in length, displays outsized ears. The gray fox is also called the tree fox because of its unique climbing ability. In the bottom row (left) is the Arctic fox, seen in its dark silvery-blue summer coat. In winter this fox's fur may turn almost completely white, becoming an effective camouflage as it hunts. The startled-looking fellow in the center, dubbed "silver fox" in the fur trade, is actually a color mutant of the North American red fox. With its oversized ears, the big-eared fox of Africa (right) resembles the fennec, but at 20 inches long it is considerably larger than its northern cousin. At the far right is the stilt-legged maned wolf of tropical South America, a solitary, shy fox-like canid that steers clear of man and his livestock.

Fennec

Arctic fox

"Silver fox"

Gray fox

Big-eared fox

Maned wolf

109

THE BIOGRAPHY OF AN
ARCTIC FOX

by Ernest Thompson Seton

Ernest Thompson Seton (1860–1946) probably introduced more young readers to the world of nature than any other writer of his time. In the selection below, from The Biography of an Arctic Fox, *Seton describes the arduous courtship of a male Arctic fox that he names Katug, which first has to locate a mate, the alluring little vixen, Laigu, then fight off a rival and finally win Laigu with a succulent gift before consummating the union. As in all his writings, whether for adults or youngsters, Seton is meticulously accurate in his descriptions.*

Seventy times seven he had sung, and now the slow response a mile away in the half-night, a long shrill note. Seabirds might have passed it for a Seabird wail. Polar Hares might have taken it for an ice-cake flood-pushed on the rocks. Caribou might have thought it the scraping of willow twig on twig. A Mouse might have said, "My far-off brother has a little cold to-night." But Katug made no errors in his guess, and he raced with his keen black nose aloft and his keen brown eyes aglow.

You must have noticed each time you land in summer on any part of the Polar realm that you soon find animal life, and having found one creature, are not long in discovering another near-by. For the wild things are sociable, and hermits are rare among them.

So Katug's keen night-eyes, when he had come to the place of the voice, scanning the brown dune sides, picked at once on a whitish blot behind a willow scrub, and swung to windward of it. But as he swung, another white thing showed up against the leaden sky. It moved a little, and the telltale wind brought wireless words that told him of a truth that here and near were two more Foxes, Foxes of his kind—one male and the other a desirable mate.

This is Nature's eternal triangle; but she solves it quickly, does not let it dawdle long. This only Katug knew: Here is a most alluring female, not unwilling, because she answered to his cry; but here is another male who has aspirations at least, maybe rights, and maybe stronger than himself. How may he find the truth?

Safe instincts had Katug, that should solve the riddle.

He stood up square, erect on a ridge, and yapped the wailing old song. Then the rival on the other ridge stood square and yapped the same.

The peace disturber behind the willow scrub lay still, but she flopped her tail just once. Then Katug walked slowly, stiffly forward, standing high; and as he did, the rival too came walking. Now, by all good rules, had they been mated, the female should at this juncture have gone quickly to her husband's side. But she lay still, and gave no sign except that tantalizing tail-flop.

The rival Foxes neared each other; doubtless their slow approach was meant for dignity, but it looked much like caution. When five hops apart, they stopped, stared, then slowly circled, so each in turn got all the information that the wind could give. Then they faced each other; each ready but unwilling to begin. Stock-still they stood, for ten heart-beats or more.

Then the tail in the willow scrub flopped.

The rivals snarled and forward marched, presenting each to the other the shoulder and, high-hung over it, the big white tail. They glanced sideways, chattered and

snarled and feinted, and then closed. Their slender legs were kept out of harm's way, their gleaming teeth found only the deep fur and tooth-proof skin of the neck.

The onset was little more than the buffing together of two feather pillows; but in a few sharp bumps, the stranger Fox went down, and Katug stood above him, snarling, with every ivory tooth displayed. Katug did not set foot on his rival; that is not done, because it gives the rival a chance to snap at his foot, the most easily injured part of all. But he stood snarling at him. For a little while the stranger lay; then, seeming to get back his breath, leaped up. Again they went at it. But Katug had the overweight, and downed the stranger as before. Three times they closed in bloodless fight; and three times downed, the stranger sprang to his feet and fled.

And the white tail in the willow scrub went flip, flop.

With tremendous dignity, Katug stared, as his rival skulked away. Then with one less degree of dignity, he walked, stalked toward the willow scrub. The lady Fox arose and moved so that the willow was between. He passed around it, and she bounded away. He followed and overtook her, but she faced him with a rōw of threatening teeth.

Now Katug knew by the testimony of his every sense that here was indeed the elixir for all his woes. He was ablaze with hope and yearning. She continued to run and he to overtake her, but there was no acceptance in her hostile face. They dodged about and kept up the comic warfare for a long time. Then, puzzled, Katug lay down on the ground, and the lady lay down too—at a safe distance.

Thus he waited for a while; but a glimpse of the defeated rival watching from a neighboring ridge, set him astir. He again approached the charmer. He made little foxy whines. He stopped and crouched on the ground. She retreated slowly. Two rocks offered a sort of bay. Into this she backed and faced about as he slowly neared. He whined, she snarled and showed her teeth.

Katug backed away and sank down. She crouched in the rocky corner. As he sprawled, a Lemming, a Snow-mouse, rustled under the near tangle. He sprang on it and held it warm, crushed and bloody, in his jaws. He crawled slowly up to the crouching she-one. He laid the Lemming down at her feet then backed away to watch. She hesitated, then slowly reached her slim white nose, took the blood-warm tidbit, chopped it a little to make its richness flow, then swallowed it blissfully.

"Every she-Fox has her price," or something like that said a certain cynic. This one's price was one fat Lemming, at least it seemed so; for when next Katug ventured forward, she made no move, but lay low, crouching, as he deferentially approached and gently licked her nose, her ears, her head. She made no move, she made no sound at first. But soon gave answer with a tiny inward purring.

This was the wedding of Katug and Liagu.

Weasels and Their Kin

Among the lesser known and most intriguing of the hunting mammals are the weasels, a large and ancient group that ranges over much of the world. Land weasels vary in size from the tiny two-ounce least weasel—the smallest of all carnivores—to the legendary and much-feared wolverine, a bearlike animal of up to 60 pounds. The family includes such diversely adapted predators as the badger, a chunky, powerful digger that can tunnel through the ground at the rate of several feet a minute to overtake a prairie dog; the sea and river otters, sleek, playful swimmers that can stay under water for long periods in pursuit of fish and other prey; and the marten, an agile climber and leaper that moves easily for miles through treetops to catch red squirrels, its favorite game.

Weasels are members of the family Mustelidae, or mustelids. The name comes from the strong-scented must, or musk, produced by highly specialized anal glands. A mustelid's distinctive odor is useful in many ways: to mark the location of buried meat for later consumption or to make it unappetizing to other animals; to attract mates; to identify its territory; to warn trespassers; and to discourage attack from enemies. The most notoriously effective in deploying these glands for self-defense is the skunk, which can direct a burst of yellow acidic liquid accurately at targets up to 12 feet away.

Other members of the tribe can count on some help from their odor, but most depend on other attributes to stay alive. The smallest species—the least, short-tail and long-tail weasels—are slim, almost snakelike little animals that move quickly and can slip into small holes and crevices to escape predators or to hunt mice and voles. Establishing dens under rocks or woodpiles or in abandoned rabbit holes, they mate in summer, but through the phenomenon of delayed implantation (see page 20) the young are not born until well into the spring of the following year, when winter is over and they have the best chance of surviving.

These three weasels also change color for seasonal camouflage. A rich brown summer coat is replaced by a thicker winter white when the weather begins to turn cold. This has been a mixed blessing for the short-tail weasel, whose winter fur—known as ermine—has long been highly prized for elegant capes and stoles.

The prospect of winding up as a fur coat has proven even more of a threat to the mink, whose luxuriant chocolate-brown coat is useful to its original owner because it keeps it warm and dry during its excursions into ponds and streams to feed on frogs, fish and crustaceans. The mink's most formidable prey is the muskrat, a water-dwelling rodent and an excellent swimmer.

While the mink was evolving into a watergoing weasel, its slightly larger cousin the marten solved the problem of competition for food by specializing in aggressive aerial acrobatics, racing with astounding speed and balance through dense canopies of spruce, fir and hemlock in pursuit of prey. Like a close relative, the Russian sable, martens have been much reduced in numbers by being trapped for their beautiful dark pelts.

A larger version of the marten, weighing up to 20 pounds, is the Pennant's marten, more often called the fisher or fisher cat. It is neither fisher nor cat, though fishers are almost equally at home in trees and water. They prey on frogs and muskrats, chipmunks and squirrels, and when food is scarce they have been known to take foxes, beavers and even young or winter-weakened deer. The specialty on the fisher's menu, however, is an animal most others do not dare touch—the bristly quilled porcupine, which the fisher deftly unseats from a tree branch and flips over; then, avoiding most of the spines, it attacks the unprotected belly.

The fisher's worst enemy is man, who has drastically cut back its forest domain for farms and lumber and has trapped it relentlessly for its beautiful blackish, frosty-haired fur, which once brought well over $100 a pelt. Reduced to a rarity in many places, the fisher has made something of a comeback in Vermont and other areas. In these regions, animals trapped elsewhere have been released; they have multiplied and serve to control the porcupine, which destroys timber by eating bark.

The most fearsome hunter of the weasel family is unquestionably the wolverine, whose fate is even more precarious than that of the fisher. The wolverine has been hunted, trapped and forced back into the wilderness as a supposed threat to man, game and livestock. Today wolverines inhabit only remote parts of Canada, Alaska and northern Eurasia.

Variously referred to as the glutton, skunk bear, devil bear and demon of the north, the wolverine has acquired a formidable reputation. Indeed, the animal, which looks like a small, short-legged bear with a bushy tail, is astonishingly strong and persistent. On Mount McKinley in Alaska, naturalists saw a wolverine kill a mountain sheep more than three times its weight and transport the body a mile and a half over steep, snowy terrain and across a river before finding a suitable place for lunch.

Black-footed ferret

Pine marten

Striped skunk

Canadian river otter

Fisher

Badger

115

Water Weasels

Born naked, blind and helpless, young minks (above) are more dependent than most members of the weasel family. By the time they are six or seven weeks old, however, the young minks are weaned and ready to go stalking on their own. For their 16- to 28-inch length and up to one- to three-and-a-half-pound weight, adult minks are ferocious, oftentimes killing a larger animal than they can consume. An occasional marshland sight is the carcass of a mink victim, left untouched, perhaps to be eaten later. In season, minks gorge on fish, crayfish, ducks and ducklings, and when muskrats are abundant, minks will often feed exclusively on this relatively formidable prey.

As is often the case with small hunting animals, minks sometimes suffer a turn of the predatory tables; they are particularly vulnerable to swooping attacks by hawks. But the danger is lethal only when a mink is far from water; when it is nearby, a mink can escape by diving in and staying submerged.

Furs for All Seasons

The weasel—called a stoat in Europe—is relatively safe from man in the warmer months, when it wears a rather sparse, lightweight coat that has little commercial value. But as the autumn days grow short, a new, thick, creamy winter coat called ermine replaces the summer fur, and the little creature (left) becomes an endangered species. Along with the coats of the weasel's cousins, the Russian sable and the mink, ermine is one of the most sought-after fashion furs. The pine marten (below) has an even more precarious existence than the weasel: Its brown coat remains the same color all year, an expensive fur for all seasons.

RIVERBY

by John Burroughs

In the tradition of Thoreau, naturalist John Burroughs wrote simple, descriptive essays about animal life in the back country of New England and upstate New York. In the selection below, excerpted from Riverby, *Burroughs recounts his discovery of the den of a busy weasel. At first he is content to watch the lithe little creature stock its larder, but eventually his scientific curiosity gets the better of him, and he decides to investigate the weasel's underground hideaway. What he unearths is impressive, but in the end Burroughs regrets his intrusion.*

My most interesting note of the season of 1893 relates to a weasel. One day in early November, my boy and I were sitting on a rock at the edge of a tamarack swamp in the woods, hoping to get a glimpse of some grouse which we knew were in the habit of feeding in the swamp. We had not sat there very long before we heard a slight rustling in the leaves below us, which we at once fancied was made by the cautious tread of a grouse. (We had no gun.) Presently, through the thick brushy growth, we caught sight of a small animal running along that we at first took for a red squirrel. A moment more, and it came into full view but a few yards from us, and we saw that it was a weasel. A second glance showed that it carried something in its mouth which, as it drew near, we saw was a mouse or a mole of some sort. The weasel ran nimbly along, now the

length of a decayed log, then over stones and branches, pausing a moment every three or four yards, and passed within twenty feet of us and disappeared behind some rocks on the bank at the edge of the swamp. "He is carrying food into his den," I said, "let us watch him." In four or five minutes he reappeared, coming back over the course along which he had just passed, running over and under the same stones and down the same decayed log, and was soon out of sight in the swamp. We had not moved, and evidently he had not noticed us. After about six minutes we heard the same rustle as at first, and in a moment saw the weasel coming back with another mouse in his mouth. He kept to his former route as if chained to it, making the same pauses and gestures and repeating exactly his former movements. He disappeared on our left as before, and after a few moments' delay re-emerged and took his course down into the swamp again. We waited about the same length of time as before, when back he came with another mouse. He evidently had a big crop of mice down there amid the bogs and bushes, and he was gathering his harvest in very industriously. We became curious to see exactly where his den was, and so walked around where he had seemed to disappear each time, and waited. He was as punctual as usual and was back with his game exactly on time. It happened that we had stopped within two paces of his hole, so that, as he approached it, he evidently discovered us. He paused, looked steadily at us, and then without any sign of fear entered his den. The

entrance was not under the rocks as we had expected, but was in the bank a few feet beyond them. We remained motionless for some time, but he did not reappear. Our presence had made him suspicious and he was going to wait awhile. Then I removed some dry leaves and exposed his doorway, a small, round hole, hardly as large as the chipmunk makes, going straight down into the ground. We had a lively curiosity to get a peep into his larder. If he had been carrying in mice at this rate very long, his cellars must be packed with them. With a sharp stick I began digging into the red clayey soil but soon encountered so many roots from near trees that I gave it up, deciding to return next day with a mattock. So I repaired the damages I had done as well as I could, replaced the leaves, and we moved off.

The next day, which was mild and still as usual, I came back armed, as I thought, to unearth the weasel and his treasures. I sat down where we had sat the day before and awaited developments. I was curious to know if the weasel was still carrying in his harvest. I had sat but a few minutes when I heard again the rustle in the dry leaves and saw the weasel coming home with another mouse. I observed him till he had made three trips; about every six or seven minutes, I calculated he brought in a mouse. Then I went and stood near his hole. This time he had a fat meadow mouse. He laid it down near the entrance, went in and turned around, and reached out and drew the mouse in after him. That store of mice I am bound to see, I thought,

and then fell to with the heavy mattock. I followed the hole down about two feet, when it turned to the north. I kept the clew by thrusting into the passage slender twigs; these it was easy to follow. Two or three feet more and the hole branched, one part going west, the other northeast. I followed the west one a few feet till it branched. Then I turned to the easterly tunnel and pursued it till it branched. I followed one of these ways till it divided. I began to be embarrassed and hindered by the accumulations of loose soil. Evidently this weasel had foreseen just such an assault upon his castle as I was making and had planned it accordingly. He was not to be caught napping. I found several enlargements in the various tunnels, breathing spaces, or spaces to turn around in, or to meet and chat with a companion, but nothing that looked like a terminus, a permanent living room. I tried removing the soil a couple of paces away with the mattock, but found it slow work. I was getting warm and tired, and my task was apparently only just begun. The farther I dug, the more numerous and intricate became the passages. I concluded to stop and come again the next day, armed with a shovel in addition to the mattock.

Accordingly, I came back on the morrow and fell to work vigorously. I soon had quite a large excavation; I found the bank a labyrinth of passages, with here and there a large chamber. One of the latter I struck only six inches under the surface, by making a fresh breach a few feet away.

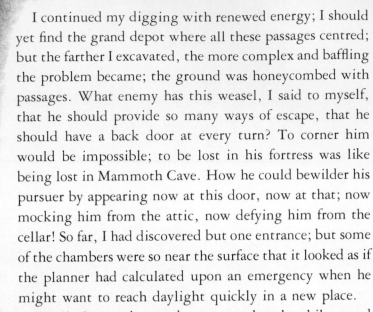

I continued my digging with renewed energy; I should yet find the grand depot where all these passages centred; but the farther I excavated, the more complex and baffling the problem became; the ground was honeycombed with passages. What enemy has this weasel, I said to myself, that he should provide so many ways of escape, that he should have a back door at every turn? To corner him would be impossible; to be lost in his fortress was like being lost in Mammoth Cave. How he could bewilder his pursuer by appearing now at this door, now at that; now mocking him from the attic, now defying him from the cellar! So far, I had discovered but one entrance; but some of the chambers were so near the surface that it looked as if the planner had calculated upon an emergency when he might want to reach daylight quickly in a new place.

Finally I paused, rested upon my shovel awhile, eased my aching back upon the ground, and then gave it up, feeling as I never had before the force of the old saying, that you cannot catch a weasel asleep. I had made an ugly hole

This swamp, maybe, had been his hunting ground for many years, and he had added another hall to his dwelling each year. After further digging I struck at least one of his banqueting halls, a cavity about the size of one's hat, arched over by a network of fine tree roots. The occupant evidently lodged or rested here also. There was a warm, dry nest, made of leaves and the fur of mice and moles. I took out two or three handfuls. In finding this chamber I had followed one of the tunnels around till it brought me within a foot of the original entrance. A few inches to one side of this cavity there was what I took to be a back alley where the weasel threw his waste; there were large masses of wet, decaying fur here, and fur pellets such as are regurgitated by hawks and owls. In the nest there was the tail of a flying squirrel, showing that the weasel sometimes had a flying squirrel for supper or dinner.

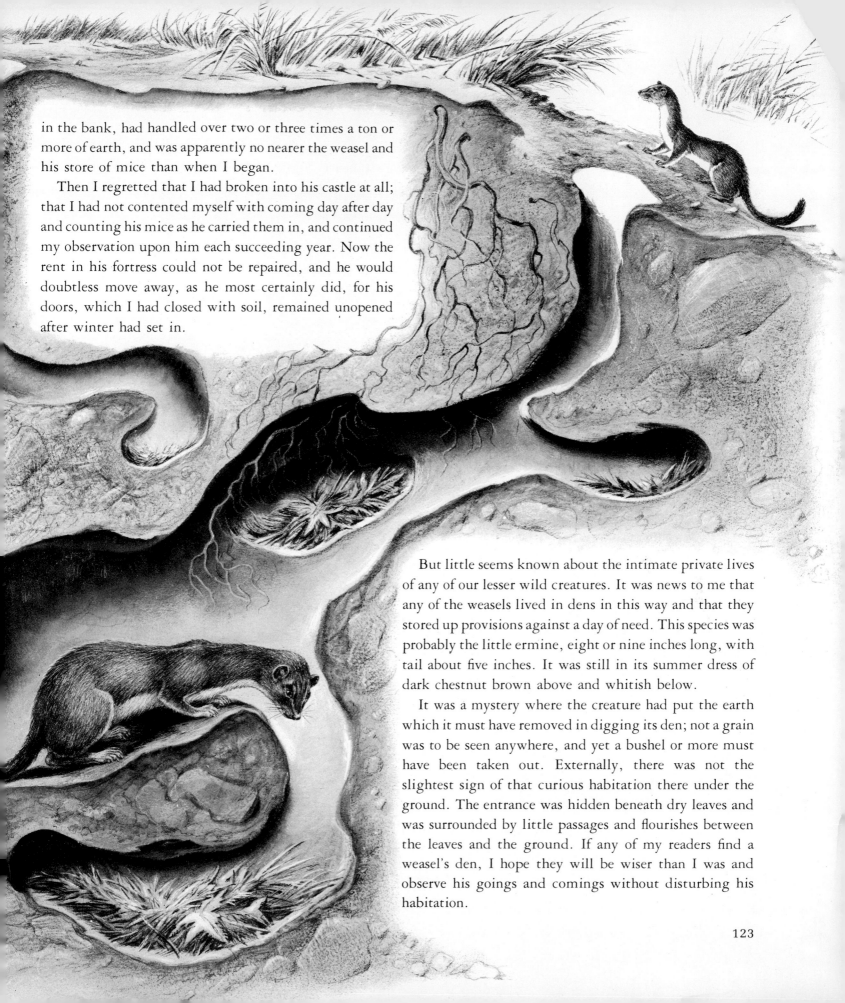

in the bank, had handled over two or three times a ton or more of earth, and was apparently no nearer the weasel and his store of mice than when I began.

Then I regretted that I had broken into his castle at all; that I had not contented myself with coming day after day and counting his mice as he carried them in, and continued my observation upon him each succeeding year. Now the rent in his fortress could not be repaired, and he would doubtless move away, as he most certainly did, for his doors, which I had closed with soil, remained unopened after winter had set in.

But little seems known about the intimate private lives of any of our lesser wild creatures. It was news to me that any of the weasels lived in dens in this way and that they stored up provisions against a day of need. This species was probably the little ermine, eight or nine inches long, with tail about five inches. It was still in its summer dress of dark chestnut brown above and whitish below.

It was a mystery where the creature had put the earth which it must have removed in digging its den; not a grain was to be seen anywhere, and yet a bushel or more must have been taken out. Externally, there was not the slightest sign of that curious habitation there under the ground. The entrance was hidden beneath dry leaves and was surrounded by little passages and flourishes between the leaves and the ground. If any of my readers find a weasel's den, I hope they will be wiser than I was and observe his goings and comings without disturbing his habitation.

123

A Scrappy Heavyweight

The wolverine is, pound for pound, the strongest and fiercest of the weasels and is the most pugnacious among the 70 species that constitute the mustelid family. Solidly built with its 60-pound weight and three-foot length, the wolverine can deliver a bone-crushing bite that makes it capable of defeating a lone wolf, though it rightly fears a wolf pack. But the wolverine lives up to its ferocious reputation only in the winter. With its large, broad feet, webbed between the toes, serving as snowshoes, the wolverine is able to run speedily, silently and tirelessly across country, overtaking deer, foxes, hares, squirrels and occasionally a moose or an elk.

In the summer, however, the wolverine's predatory ways are restricted. Without thick snow to muffle its heavy footsteps, the animal's progress is too noisy for efficient hunting. During the warmer months the wolverine must make do with carrion, the eggs of ground-nesting birds and insect larvae, as well as berries, fruits and nuts.

Like most mustelids, wolverines are territorial animals. Male wolverines share vast ranges, which can cover up to half a million acres, with only one or two females. The territories are marked with a combination of feces, urine and glandular secretions. These territories are guarded closely. In fact, a wolverine's young, considered potential interlopers, are allowed to remain inside the male's domain for only their first two years. Soon thereafter they are driven out and forced to establish areas of their own.

Although wolverines are powerful tree-climbers (left) and have been known to chase lynxes into trees, they more often pursue their prey on the ground. They hunt primarily by scent, but their senses of sight and hearing are also well developed. Wolverines usually kill smaller prey by biting their necks and snapping the spinal cord. In winter they are sometimes able to jump on larger animals from behind, ride them and bite them on the nape of the neck until they fall.

Credits

Cover—Nina Leen. 1—Charles Summers, Jr., from Amwest. 5—Bullaty Lomeo from Rapho Division, Photo Researchers, Inc. 6—(left) Rolf O. Peterson, (right) S. Wayman, Time, Inc. 7—Co Rentmeester, Time, Inc. 9—G. R. Martin from Bruce Coleman, Inc. 15—Mike Luque. 16–17—Tom Bledsoe from Photo Researchers, Inc., 17—Charles Summers, Jr., from Colorado Nature Photographic Studio. 18—Tom Bledsoe from Photo Researchers, Inc. 19—(top) Leonard Lee Rue III from Photo Researchers, Inc., (bottom) Tom Bledsoe from Photo Researchers, Inc. 20—Tom Bledsoe from Photo Researchers, Inc. 21—(top) Mike Luque, (bottom) Tom Bledsoe from Photo Researchers, Inc. 22—D. & R. Sullivan from Bruce Coleman, Inc. 22–23—Tom McHugh from Photo Researchers, Inc. 24–25—John J. Craighead, 25—Stouffer Productions, Ltd. from Bruce Coleman, Inc. 26–27—Stouffer Productions, Ltd. from Bruce Coleman, Inc. 32—Bullaty Lomeo from Rapho Division, Photo Researchers, Inc. 33—(left) Mike Luque, (right) Tom McHugh from Photo Researchers, Inc. 34—Arthur Swoger. 35—(top and bottom) Jonathan Wright from Bruce Coleman, Inc. 36—(left) George Holton from Photo Researchers, Inc., (right) Bucky Reeves from National Audubon Society Collection, Photo Researchers, Inc. 37—(top) Russ Kinne from Photo Researchers, Inc., (bottom) D. & R. Sullivan from Bruce Coleman, Inc. 43—Fred Baldwin from Photo Researchers, Inc. 44–45—Co Rentmeester, Time, Inc. 46–47—Co Rentmeester, Time, Inc. 48—(left) B. Knudsen, (right) J. Rychetnik from Photo Researchers, Inc. 49—Jeffrey Stoll from Jacana. 50–51—Carleton Ray from Photo Researchers, Inc. 53—Russ Kinne from Photo Researchers, Inc. 54—George Holton from Photo Researchers, Inc. 55—(top) Peter Kaplan from Photo Researchers, Inc., (bottom) Norman Myers from Bruce Coleman, Inc. 57—S. Wayman, Time, Inc. 58–59—Rod Allin from Bruce Coleman, Inc. 59—S. Wayman, Photo Researchers, Inc. 60–61—Rolf O. Peterson. 62–63—Gordon Haber. 64—Rolf O. Peterson. 65—Gordon Haber. 66–67—S. Wayman from Time, Inc. 73—Oxford Scientific Films from Bruce Coleman, Inc. 74–75—George Schaller. 76–77—George Schaller from Bruce Coleman, Inc. 77—George Schaller. 79—Clem Haagner from Bruce Coleman, Inc. 80—(top) Fran Allan from Animals Animals, 80–81 (bottom) John Dominis, Time, Inc. 81—(top) Tom Nebbia from DPI. 83—Masud Quraishy from Bruce Coleman, Inc. 84–85—Norman Myers from Bruce Coleman, Inc. 86–87—Bob Campbell from Bruce Coleman, Inc. 91—John Ebeling from Photo Researchers, Inc. 92—S. Wayman from Photo Researchers, Inc. 93—(top) E. A. Heiniger from Rapho Division, Photo Researchers, Inc., (bottom) Charles Summers, Jr., from Amwest. 94—(top) S. Wayman, Time, Inc., (bottom) Nicholas Devore III from Bruce Coleman, Inc. 95—(top, left) Charles Summers, Jr., from Amwest, (top, right) J. Simon from Photo Researchers, Inc., (bottom) Tom McHugh from Wildlife Unlimited, from Photo Researchers, Inc. 96—John Ebeling from Bruce Coleman, Inc. 97—Dominick Maio. 103—Des and Jen Bartlett from Bruce Coleman, Inc. 104—John J. Craighead. 105—Jen and Des Bartlett from Bruce Coleman, Inc. 106—(left) Jen and Des Bartlett from Bruce Coleman, Inc., (right) Russ Kinne from Photo Researchers, Inc. 107—(top) L. David Mech, (bottom) Michael Smith from National Audubon Society Collection, Photo Researchers, Inc. 108—(left) S. C. Bisserot from Bruce Coleman, Inc., (top, right) Anthony Mercieca from National Audubon Society Collection, Photo Researchers, Inc., (bottom, right) J. Van Wormer from Bruce Coleman, Inc. 109—(top, left) Kirtley-Perkins from Photo Researchers, Inc., (bottom, left) Norman Myers from Bruce Coleman, Inc., (right) Norman Tomalin from Bruce Coleman, Inc. 115—(top, left) B. J. Rose, (top, right) Hans Reinhard from Bruce Coleman, Inc., (center, left) Leonard Lee Rue III from Bruce Coleman, Inc., (center, right) Hans Reinhard from Bruce Coleman, Inc., (bottom, left) Lynn Rodgers, (bottom, right) Hope Ryden from Photo Researchers, Inc. 116—Wolfgang Obst. 117—Leonard Lee Rue III from Bruce Coleman, Inc. 118–119—A. Visage from Jacana. 119—B. Ruth from Bruce Coleman, Inc. 124—Tom McHugh from Photo Researchers, Inc. 125—J. Couffer from Bruce Coleman, Inc. 128—Charles Summers, Jr., from Amwest.

Photographs on endpapers are used courtesy of Time-Life Picture Agency, Russ Kinne and Stephen Dalton of Photo Researchers, Inc., and Nina Leen.

Film sequences on pages 8 and 13 are from "Kodiak Island" and "Prairie Dog Town," programs in the Time-Life Television series *Wild, Wild World of Animals*.

MAP on page 89 is by Breck Trautwein, based on material from *Hyaena* by Hans Kruuk, published by Oxford University Press, and the map on page 96 is also by Breck Trautwein.

ILLUSTRATIONS on pages 10, 11 and 12 are by Chester Tarka; those on pages 28–29 are used by permission of the Center for Western Studies, University of the Pacific, Stockton, California, courtesy of the Muir-Hanna families. The illustration on page 31 is used by permission of the National Park Service/Yosemite Collection, courtesy of the Muir-Hanna families. The illustrations on pages 38–41, 68–71, 88–89, 98–101 and 110–113 are by John Groth; those on pages 120–123 are by André Durenceau.

Bibliography

NOTE: Asterisk at the left means that a paperback volume is also listed in *Books in Print*.

Bates, Marston, and the Editors of Time-Life Books, *The Land and Wildlife of South America*. Time-Life Books, 1964.

Bledsoe, Wade T., "The Social Life of an Unsociable Giant." *Audubon*. Vol. LXXVII, No. 3 (May 1975), pp. 2–16.

Brown, Dale, and the Editors of Time-Life Books, *Wild Alaska*. Time-Life Books, 1972.

Bueler, Lois E., *Wild Dogs of the World*. Stein and Day, 1973.

Burrows, Roger, *Wild Fox*. Taplinger, 1968.

Caras, Roger, *North American Mammals*. Meredith Press, 1967.

———, *The Custer Wolf*. Little, Brown, 1966.

*Carrighar, Sally, *One Day at Teton Marsh*. Alfred A. Knopf, 1947.

Clarkson, Ewan, *Wolf Country*. E. P. Dutton, 1975.

Cott, Hugh, *Looking at Animals: A Zoologist in Africa*. Charles Scribner's Sons, 1975.

*Crisler, Lois, *Arctic Wild*. Harper & Row, 1958.

Dudley, Ernest, *Rufus. The Remarkable Story of a Tamed Fox*. Hart Publishing Company, 1972.

Dufresne, Frank, *No Room for Bears*. Holt, Rinehart and Winston, 1965.

Egbert, Allan L., and Luque, Michael H., "Among Alaska's Brown Bears." *National Geographic*. Vol. CXLVIII, No. 3 (September 1975), pp. 428–442.

Fox, Michael, *Behavior of Wolves, Dogs and Related Canids*. Harper & Row, 1972.

Grzimek, Bernhard, *Among the Animals of Africa*. Stein and Day, 1970.

———, *Animal Life Encyclopedia*, Vol. 12. Van Nostrand Reinhold, 1975.

Haynes, Bessie Doak and Edgar, *The Grizzly Bear*. University of Oklahoma Press, 1966.

Illingworth, Frank, *Wild Life Beyond the North*. Charles Scribner's Sons, 1952.

Koch, Thomas J., *The Year of the Polar Bear*. Bobbs-Merrill, 1975.

Kruuk, Hans, *The Spotted Hyena*. University of Chicago Press, 1972.

Leakey, Louis S. B., *The Wild Realm: Animals of East Africa*. National Geographic Society, 1968.

*Lorenz, Konrad Z., *Man Meets Dog*. Houghton Mifflin, 1955.

McCracken, Harold, *The Beast That Walks Like Man*. Doubleday, 1955.

Matthews, Leonard Harrison, *The Life of Mammals*, Vol. 2. Universe Books, 1971.

Mech, L. David, *The Wolf: The Ecology and Behavior of an Endangered Species*. Natural History Press, 1970.

Moss, Cynthia, *Portraits in the Wild*. Houghton Mifflin, 1975.

*Mowat, Farley, *Never Cry Wolf*. Little, Brown, 1963.

Olsen, Jack, *Slaughter the Animals, Poison the Earth*. Simon and Schuster, 1971.

Pedersen, Alwin, *Polar Animals*. Taplinger, 1966.

Pelton, Michael R., and Burghardt, Gordon M., "Black Bears of the Smokies." *Natural History*. Vol. LXXXV, No. 1 (January 1976), pp. 54–62.

Perry, Richard, *The World of the Polar Bear*. University of Washington Press, 1966.

Ripley, S. Dillon, and the Editors of Time-Life Books, *The Land and Wildlife of Tropical Asia*. Time-Life Books, 1964.

*Rood, Ronald, *Animals Nobody Loves*. The Stephen Green Press, 1971.

Rue, Leonard Lee, *The World of the Red Fox*. J. B. Lippincott, 1969.

Rutter, Russell J., and Pimlott, Douglas H., *The World of the Wolf*. J. B. Lippincott, 1968.

Ryden, Hope, *God's Dog*. Coward, McCann and Geoghegan, 1973.

Schaller, George B., *Golden Shadows, Flying Hooves*. Alfred A. Knopf, 1973.

Seton, Ernest Thompson, *The Lives of Game Animals*. Doubleday, Doran, 1929.

Stefansson, V., *The Friendly Arctic*. The Macmillan Company, 1943.

Van Lawick, Hugo, *Solo. The Story of an African Wild Dog*. Houghton Mifflin, 1974.

Van Lawick-Goodall, Hugo and Jane, *Innocent Killers*. Houghton Mifflin, 1971.

Index

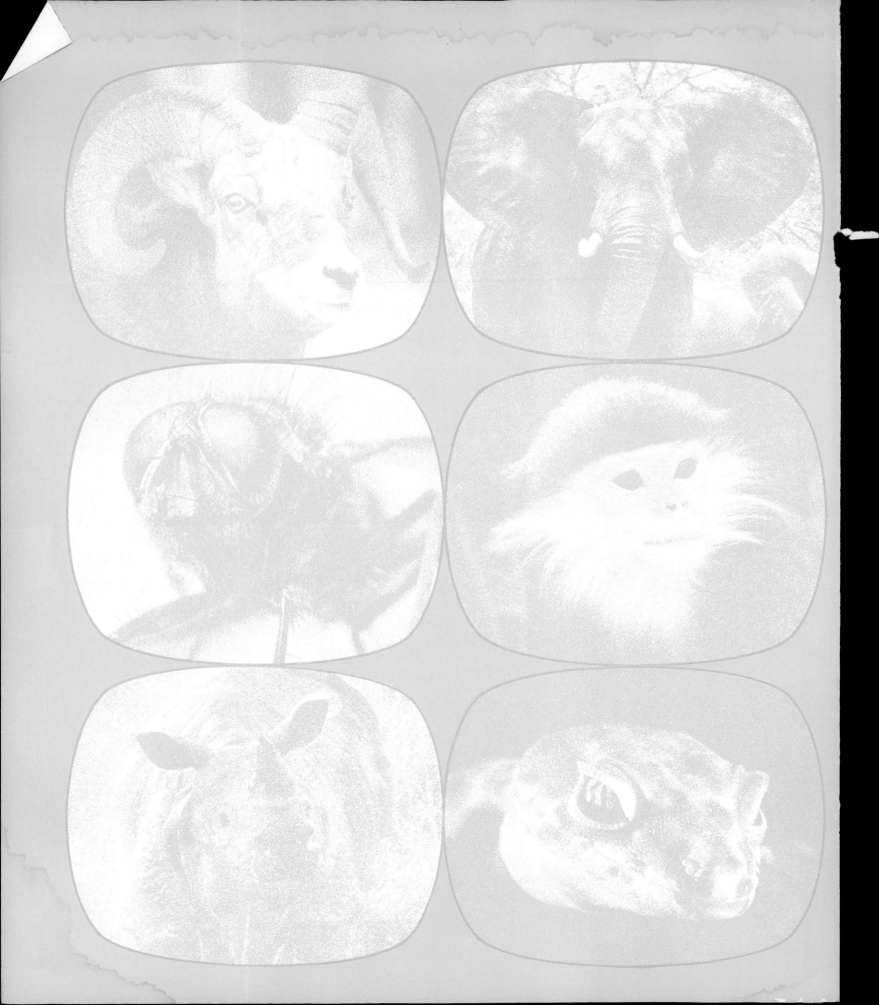